A Gift of Friendship

S I M O N & S C H U S T E R

New York London Toronto Sydney Tokyo Singapore

Women Make the Best Friends

A Celebration

—◊—

LOIS WYSE

ILLUSTRATIONS BY PAULA MUNCK

Simon & Schuster
Rockefeller Center
1230 Avenue of the Americas
New York, NY 10020

Designed by BONNI LEON-BERMAN

Manufactured in the United States of America
1 3 5 7 9 10 8 6 4 2

Library of Congress Cataloging-in-Publication Data
Wyse, Lois.
Women make the best friends : a celebration / Lois Wyse.
p. cm.
1. Women— Literary collections.   I. Title.
PN 6071.W7W97 1995
814'.54—dc20   95-33056 CIP
ISBN 0-684-80188-4

For the friends life has given me,
and for the life friends
have given me

. . . Love and thanks

Contents

THE SEASONS OF FRIENDSHIP

67

THE QUILTING BEE
LIVES
127

∽

Women Make
the Best Friends

Introduction

ALL THAT REALLY MATTERS

Your boss is mad; your spouse is complaining; the kids are cranky; and you just discovered that the roof is leaking. There's only one thing to do. Pick up the phone and call a friend.

After all, who but a good friend would put her life on hold in order to listen, advise, sympathize, and send you on your way secure in the knowledge that someone cares?

A good friend is a connection to life—a tie to the past, a road to the future, the key to sanity in a totally insane world.

Of course, friends are nothing new for us. Even the old-

17

fashioned quilting bee was a neighborly gathering of women with the ostensible purpose of bringing together patches of fabric in order to sew quilts. But with their heads bent over their work, the women at the quilting bee managed not only to sew quilts but to mend lives.

Back then a special friend or two was enough to see you through. Today most of us readily admit that we need a whole support system of loving friends.

Need is the mother of friendship, and the answer to need is the lullaby of friendship.

Who doesn't remember (and may still cherish) a first friend?

Of course, not every friendship lasts a lifetime. But the wonderful thing is that the music of those first friendships is always playing somewhere in the background as we go to other dances, other parties. Along the way we may land on a partner's toes, make an occasional misstep—or fail to hear the music. Even in friendship most of us are human, not perfect.

Friendship requires tolerance and understanding; sometimes good friends have bad days. And sometimes best friends have baggage that we fail to appreciate.

We may have friends with political beliefs that are wildly

different from ours, or who expect us to accept spouses we can't stand, or who ask advice with problems we can't solve.

But we shrug off those imperfections because these people are our friends, and this is how they come packaged.

And dear friends, no matter how we find them, are as essential to our lives as breathing in and breathing out.

When the willow bends at the first hint of troubled breezes, our friends come running to see how they can help.

Sometimes friends know when they are needed even before we realize it ourselves, because we are accustomed to letting them in on the happenings of our lives. Similarly, they trust and confide in us. We dissect, inspect, and respect all our relationships—and give both welcome and unwelcome advice to one another. We know about each other's troubled kids, troubling parents, and shaky marriages because our friends share their concerns and their triumphs. We don't keep too many secrets from true friends.

The quilting bee lives.

But now with our lives fuller, busier, and more complicated than ever, it takes more than one quilting bee to serve our life's needs. We are a society on the move, so we can't always assemble the circle we want when we want it. We find that we need different friends and different circles at different times.

So, whenever necessary, we pick up the unfinished pieces of the life we're sewing and move on to the next quilting bee. We try not to drop any stitches along the way.

Our best friends are the ones who pack easily and travel well on the road of life.

There are the old friends we cherish (even though we may rarely see one another), friends from neighborhoods, work, school, children, reading groups, bridge, tennis, the gym— and on and on and on. And in each circle we, just like the members of the quilting bee, lift our heads from the work at hand to share the secrets of our lives and loves.

This is a book of secrets, shared secrets made from the bits of life each of us brings to the quilting bee. Here are the truths we tell as we patch together the shared experiences that become the warm, rich blanket of friendship.

Most of us in the quilting bee are women, but we also open the circle and our hearts to men. After all, friendship is the prelude to love, and the love that includes friendship is the strongest love of all.

And so, when we bare our souls and tell the stories of bad

bosses, sagging roofs, crying kids and moping mates, we are really asking others to share our lives and our love. For even as we tell our stories of life gone wrong, we know we are on the way to patching our quilts.

We know because our friends listen, advise, and then promise us everything will come out just fine.

Most of all, we know in our hearts that good things will happen because we have friends willing to light the dark passages and rejoice with us at the end of the long, hard journey.

In sunshine and in sorrow, we look for those who will always stand with us.

And we know all that really matters is that we are not alone so long as we can call one person *friend*.

First Friends

CHOICES

Did I choose you?
Did you choose me?
And what difference does it make?
All that really matters, friend,
Is that we chose
Together.

A New World

Five-year-old Brooke held her doll tightly as she sat on the edge of her bed. From below she could hear her mother talking on the phone.

"Oh yes, Brooke is very excited about going to school," Mommy was saying. "I think nursery school was wonderful preparation for kindergarten, because she is confident and feels so good about herself. She really has been a leader in her preschool class."

Brooke put her hands over her ears to shut out the words.

Mommy just didn't understand anything. There she was drinking her coffee and talking about how good Brooke felt. Didn't Mommy know that Brooke was up in her room clutching her best doll because she was scared down to her socks? Who wouldn't be? She'd worked so hard to be the best in her pre-K reading readiness group, and she finally was beginning to color inside the lines instead of letting her colors spill all over the pages. And now, just when it was all working out, and she was beginning to feel good about school—now they were taking her out of her nice little school and sending her to the big school with the kindergarten at the end of the street. It was enough to make a girl throw up.

Not that she hadn't thought about that, too. If she had a stomachache, Mommy wouldn't let her go to school today. But then she'd have to go tomorrow, and everybody would have picked a friend by then. Yes, that was the real problem. Brooke wasn't just leaving her familiar classroom; she was also leaving her two best friends. Katya and Danielle were not going to the public school on the corner. They were going to different schools, and she'd probably never see them again. Mommy kept saying of course the girls will get together, but Brooke still worried.

Brooke folded her arms across her middle. Her stomach

hurt. Her head hurt, too. Should she tell Mommy? Should she say she was sick? No, no, she reminded herself. She knew why she had to be there today. She had to do it, and she had to do it now.

Brooke got up slowly from the floor, went to the table in the corner of her room and smoothed out a piece of white, lined paper. Then she opened the drawer of her play table and searched for a blue crayon. She would try to do this in her best lettering ever. She steadied her hand, and in bold blue letters, she wrote:

I LOVE YOU. LOVE, BROOKE

Then she folded the paper carefully and took it downstairs.

"Are you ready for school?" Mommy asked as she put her coffee cup in the sink.

"Yes," Brooke said.

Mommy turned around to look at Brooke. "What's that in your hand, honey?"

"A letter."

"To Katy or Danielle?"

"No, it's not for them, it's for my new best friend."

29

"And who is that, dear?"

"I don't know," Brooke answered forlornly. "I haven't met her yet."

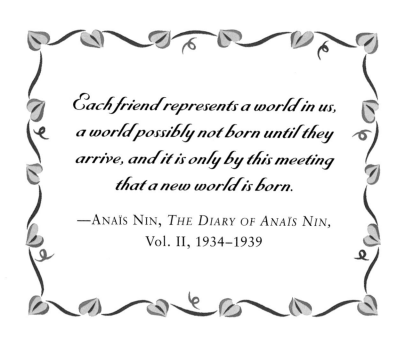

Each friend represents a world in us, a world possibly not born until they arrive, and it is only by this meeting that a new world is born.

—ANAÏS NIN, *THE DIARY OF ANAÏS NIN,* Vol. II, 1934–1939

For Ever and Ever

Almost all her long life Polly had hated going to birthday parties. She knew why she hated them, too. At the age of six, she had gone to Betty Lou Turner's birthday celebration, and in reaching for her piece of birthday cake, she had overturned a bowl of strawberry ice cream, and as it dribbled down the front of her party dress, everybody had laughed. Embarrassed and angered, Polly had said defiantly that birthday parties were silly, and nothing since had caused her to change her mind.

But now her son, Herbert Junior, and his wife, Lana, were going to give a birthday party for her. Oh, she'd tried to talk them out of it. She had managed to avoid a party for her sixtieth and another for her sixty-fifth. She'd even managed to skitter out of a seventieth celebration that they'd planned. But seventy-five was a diamond jubilee, Lana reminded her, and they felt she owed this celebration to the family. They were dragging her reluctantly into her dotage, she thought.

Herbert Junior kept telling her she'd have a wonderful time—all those old friends reunited. She didn't say a word about the ones who couldn't come back, the ones dead before their time. But as the date for the party approached Polly found that, despite her reluctance, she really was looking forward to seeing some of the old gang. Just think of it! Old neighbors and friends were coming all the way back here to Kansas just to celebrate with her. Herbert's biggest thrill came from telling his mother that Cora, her very oldest friend, was coming. Polly couldn't believe that Cora would actually fly from that fancy retirement community in California where she lived—one of those places where big gates kept the good folks in and the robbers out, or however it was they thought about such stuff. Just the thought of seeing Cora again sent a thrill of girlish excitement through Polly, the feeling of anticipation that had been missing from her life for years.

After all, Cora and she were oldest, best friends—even though they hadn't seen one another for twenty years. When was the last time? Must have been when Cora lost her son to cancer. Hard to believe that it was twenty years since Polly had flown to California to be with her. Well, wasn't showing up for the bad times the mark of real friends? When you grew up in a small town, as Cora and Polly had, you knew about bereavements and sending food and helping out in the kitchen. But you just didn't think quite so much effort was needed for friends for the good times. Polly wasn't sure it would have even occurred to her to invite Cora to this party.

It turned out that Cora's only possible airline connection brought her to town just an hour before the party, so Herbert and Lana went out to the airport with Polly to pick her up. "We're going right to the party," Lana explained, but it scarcely mattered to the two women in the backseat, who couldn't stop talking. Yes, Cora's daughter Ruth was doing just fine, and it was kind of incredible to comprehend, but that little baby Ruth was going to be a grandmother by Christmas. Where are the Blacks? Do you ever hear from the Breckenridges? They exchanged the latest news of their long, shared lives. And, as they did, each would steal a glance at the other. "You look pretty good for a kid your age," Polly said, laughing, and Cora put her hand on Polly's. "You look so pretty today, but when I look at you what I really see is a little girl in a white dress. Remember Betty Lou's birthday party when you spilled your plate of strawberry ice cream all over your dress?"

"Why do you think I bought this white dress?" Polly answered. "I knew you'd be the only one who'd understand. I can probably be trusted not to spill the ice cream today."

Their eyes met, and they laughed.

The long table was filled with family and the friends, "my Johnny-come-lately friends," Polly said, "because most of you have known me only thirty or forty years. But dear Cora at the other end of the table—well, Cora has been my best friend since we were four."

"That's true," Cora said, and then as the room went silent, Cora stood and raised her glass. "Polly has always been a true friend. Even though we don't often see one another, I remember her in my thoughts and prayers. And now I want to tell you something, Polly. You have always been very precious to me, and I hold the memory of your friendship in my heart. And in all these years, through marriage and other friendships, I have never told our secret to another person."

Polly pushed her chair back and faced her friend. Then she lifted her glass and looking down the table said softly, "Nor have I."

Herbert looked at Lana and was surprised to see that his wife's eyes were filled with tears.

Lana shook her head in a kind of wonderment, "What

could the secret be?" she whispered to her husband.

"It doesn't matter," Herbert replied.

Herbert knew what really mattered at this moment was the overwhelming love he felt for his mother, and although he knew his heart was brimming, he didn't know that tears were rolling down his cheeks, too.

I want to be your friend
For ever and ever without break or decay.
When the hills are all flat
And the rivers are all dry,
When it lightens and thunders
in winter,
When it rains and snows in summer,
When Heaven and Earth mingle
Not till then will I part from you.

—"OATHS OF FRIENDSHIP,"
CHINESE, FIRST CENTURY A.D.

$\mathcal{A}\ Second\ Self$

Victor bit his lip as he pushed back the draperies and anxiously looked up the street for a sign of Gwen's red Thunderbird. She would have plenty of explaining to do once she came home. Three years they'd been married now. Three years that had been good. Perfect? Hardly. But then, what was? Certainly not his first marriage to Kay. He hadn't ever really told Gwen all the reasons he'd left Kay. They were too painful. He turned his back to the window. Oh God. Just to think of Kay made him sick. Unfaithful. That's the word that always stayed with him. Unfaithful Kay. And now Gwen. It was—

"Victor, what are you doing home so early?" Gwen smiled that crooked little half smile that always captivated him, dropped her keys on the table, and came over to kiss him.

He'd been so preoccupied he hadn't even heard Gwen's car come into the drive, hadn't heard her key in the lock, and now even the smile didn't move him.

"Victor dear, what's the matter? Are you all right?" Gwen, like a concerned mother with a sick child, reached to feel his forehead.

Victor felt his stomach churning. He had to speak. She was acting the worried wife, and he was furious. He wheeled and spewed his words. "I'm fifty years old, Gwen, and I don't deserve to be deceived twice by women I married."

Gwen put her hand to her throat. "I don't know what you're talking about. Deceive you? We haven't spent a night apart since we were married three years ago. And before that—"

"That's not what I'm talking about. You know what I mean."

"No, Victor, I don't." She sank into a chair.

"All right, then listen to this," Victor said in disgust. "I came home from work early to surprise you. I was going to take you out to dinner tonight, and I played the messages on the answering machine."

"What could possibly have been on that machine?" Gwen asked.

"A message from Maggie."

"How can I deceive you by getting messages from my best friend?"

"It was *what* she said. She was advising you about my daughter Kay Kay. She's recommending a drug treatment center—listen, Gwen, that is private family business. How can you betray me by telling anyone about Kay Kay's problem? She's my—"

Gwen stood and walked toward Victor. Her voice low and strong, she said, "Betray you? That's what you call betrayal? Listen, Victor. We've been married for three years. And I love you. So let's start there. But my life didn't begin the day I married you or even the day I met you. Your daughter's problem is affecting my life, too. Maggie is my best friend. Victor, for heaven's sake, what do you think women talk about? The weather? How do you think I coped so many years with an abusive first husband, divorce, single parenthood, redating, and remarrying without jumping out a window? Let me tell you how. I shared my problems with my friends."

Victor was not mollified. "Now it's time to stop," he importuned. "Now," he said sternly, "you are married. You have me."

Gwen stood up, walked to the counter, and looked him straight in the eye. "The books probably say I should be gentle with you because you've been bruised by a bad relationship, but frankly, I can't deal with all that psychological advice. I can't help what happened in your first marriage, and I'm sure I don't know everything about it. But I do know all about my friends. I know everything about them, Victor, because I've had these friends a lot longer than I've had you. And they know everything about me. They ask. I ask. We all listen. But look, my dear, if you can promise to give me two or three hours a day of your undivided attention, your total sympathetic support without criticism or sarcastic remarks or judgments, and if you can be available to me anytime I need to talk—without reading the paper or watching TV—then I'll be delighted to stop blabbing to my friends and do all my talking to you."

Victor took a deep breath. "I think we should call the center Maggie recommended," he said.

Friendship is essentially a partnership
. . . a friend is a second self. . . .

—ARISTOTLE

A Similarity of Character

Bonnie and I were on the school bus, and we were both in the third grade. It happened that we were sitting next to each other one day. There was another girl on the bus, Carla, who was acting really bossy toward some little kids. Now you have to understand that even though Bonnie and I were in the same class, we'd never actually played together. But there we were sitting together, and this girl Carla was so disgusting that I turned to Bonnie and said, 'I hate her.'

"'Me too,' Bonnie said."

"From that day to this, Bonnie and I have been best friends.

"That was forty years ago.

"And you know what? We still hate Carla."

—*A computer programmer in Encino*

. . . friendship . . . is founded not only on a similarity of character, but of condition.

—Jean-Jacques Rousseau, *Julie: Or The New Héloïse*

It's Friendship

 Corky is famous for being the friend who is always there.

At the first sniffle, it is Corky who sends the soup.

Surgery? Corky is the one with the confident smile who is cheering the family as they wait outside the operating room.

A raise? A promotion? An honor? Corky makes the first congratulatory phone call and then dials the world to spread the good news.

So when Corky called her friends and casually invited them to lunch, everyone looked forward to a good time.

Not that Corky was some mindless Mary Sunshine. After all, she did have her share of ups and downs while raising her children, but, as partners in a solid and happy marriage, she and her husband had weathered them all.

At lunch Corky turned to her friends. "I have something to tell you," she said quietly.

Her strangely serious manner silenced the women's conversations at the table.

"I have some news about me I want to share with you," Corky said in her usual crisp tone and then went on, "I have lymphoma, but it has been found early, so I'm sure that I'll be all right. I want all of you to know that I am getting treatment, and I expect it to be completely successful. I'm telling you all at once, so that there'll be no wondering and no secrets."

Each friend reacted the same way. Stunned and numb at first, they did not wait long to go into action.

If Corky was going to fight, then her friends were going to be there to make sure she had plenty of ammunition.

Letters, cards, gifts, jokes, lunches, dinners—all the things Corky had done for others for so many years, they now did for her.

Corky couldn't believe the deluge of love and prayers. And so, six months after she was diagnosed, Corky—still confident she was headed toward remission—sent a letter to all her friends. In part it read:

"There you were and there you are. Your repeated offers of help; your notes; your gifts; your plants; your flowers; your phone calls; your messages; that which you said and that which you did not. That outpouring of caring and sharing has given me immeasurable strength coupled with insurmountable gratitude."

The letter went on.

So did the friends.

So did Corky.

She went through the painful therapies and the abysmal waiting rooms. She endured the long needles and the endless promises that didn't always come true.

And then, almost a year after the first diagnosis, the doctors told Corky she was cured.

Corky's friends were ecstatic.

Cured! That meant Corky could pick up her heavy schedule of volunteer work, play golf and party once more. What would she do first? one delighted friend asked.

"I know exactly what I am going to do now," Corky answered quietly. "I am going to take the next plane to

Jerusalem with my husband, and I am going to write the name of every friend of mine who needs prayers on a slip of paper. And then I am going to the western wall of Herod's Temple because I believe that prayers are answered when they are written and put in the cracks of the Wailing Wall. I don't know any better way to thank my friends than to pray for them."

It's friendship, friendship
Just a perfect blendship.

—COLE PORTER, "FRIENDSHIP,"
DU BARRY WAS A LADY

Old Friends

There is a time in the life of girls, between crib and boys, when horses rule the world.

For Karen and Gina, it happened at the age of eight.

The two lived on opposite ends of Long Island and were sent one summer to the same equestrian camp. From the moment they met, the two girls vowed they would be friends. Of course, they had no idea how they'd accomplish such a thing, since they truly lived a day's drive apart. And once camp was over and school began, even sleepovers would be almost impossible because each child had her own schedule of school activities and lessons.

Besides, who would ever drive either of them such a long, long way?

Sadly they bade farewell at the end of summer and promised that the next summer they would meet at camp.

Three months later Karen opened the front door, and there was Gina.

"Gina!" she shrieked. "How did you ever get here?"

"Our family moved to your street."

"I don't believe it," Karen gasped.

As neighbors for the next ten years, the girls cemented their friendship not only with their mutual love of horses, but love of learning, and love of boys, which eventually, for Gina, led to marriage and moving away.

Still, the two phoned frequently, and each year, no matter where in the world her work as a photojournalist took her, Karen went to Georgia to visit Gina and her husband. And later, after the birth of her two children, it was Gina's family that Karen loved, too.

One day Karen picked up the phone to hear Gina's husband, "It's her fortieth birthday, and I'm having a surprise party—"

Before he could finish, Karen promised to fly to Georgia to be the added surprise.

There were tears and there was laughter that night, and

Gina was beyond words of thanks when Karen gave her a painting made by Karen's grandmother, one Gina she had loved as a child.

"The rest of my gift to you," Karen promised, "is a ride into the sunrise tomorrow morning. After all, Gina, you're only forty, so it's too early to ride into the sunset. But when you do, I'll be there, too."

Things like sticking to old friends have really got bigger to me than anything else.

—SHERWOOD ANDERSON,
LETTERS OF SHERWOOD ANDERSON

In Want of Something

O n Mother's Day, Rhonda stood with the hymnal in her hand, and as she sang her thanks to God, she began to cry.

How could a good and gracious God let her and Tim sing His praises while denying them the one thing they wanted most in life, to have a child?

Tim put his arm around Rhonda, but she could not stop the tears of grief and anger. Why hadn't God answered her prayers when she knew He was the one who had put this longing to be a mother in her heart?

"Talk to Julie," Tim whispered. "She's a nurse, and she's been there for you all the way."

This had been Tim's and Rhonda's month of decision. After years of trying, after years of doctors and laboratories and effort, she awoke this morning to find that her period had started. And this was the month that was their cut-off date. After this, they had both agreed that there would be no more doctors. No more scheduling as though lovemaking were nothing more than time on the Stairmaster. No more strange-sounding procedures that were as torturous to the psyche as to the body. Not that they hadn't appreciated what had been done for them.

Julie. Poor Julie. She'd really tried. Tim was right. She'd have to meet Julie after church and tell her. It was over. All over.

Ended where it began. Here in church.

Julie and Rhonda had met when they both sang soprano in the church choir, and even though Julie was old enough to be Rhonda's mother, each understood that the heart has no age.

It wasn't long before the two women began meeting for a small supper before choir practice. Julie, a nurse practitioner, told Rhonda her favorite stories about the Impatient Patient and the Nervous One. And Rhonda countered with anecdotes about the kids she taught.

But as easily as she could tell stories about the kids, Rhonda couldn't tell Julie about the most important issue in her life. Then one summer night, as they finished their coffee, Julie said casually, "You like children so much, but you don't have any."

That broke the barrier. "It's not because we haven't tried," Rhonda snapped. Then she stopped. "Oh, I didn't mean to sound upset, but . . . oh, but . . ." Tears choked her words. She shook her head and made no sound.

That was when Rhonda, with Julie as her coach, began the years of procedures that had resulted only in failure.

And last week Rhonda had confessed, "It's all too much. This is the last try."

Now this dissapointment would be almost as hard for Julie as for Rhonda. But when she told her after church that May day, Julie refused to be downcast. Instead she comforted Rhonda and Tim once again. "Rhonda," she said, "I know that somewhere out there God has a baby for you, and I will keep my eyes and ears open as never before so that, through any connections I may have and not even be aware I have, I may help you."

The next day a woman with her own adopted baby came into the gynecologist's office where Julie worked.

How did you get the baby? Who? What? Where? Julie asked.

The mother carefully outlined the legal steps; Julie took notes and called Rhonda.

"God listens," Julie said. "Now it's up to us."

This time everything went according to plan. The following May Rhonda and Tim were cuddling their own adopted baby daughter.

"As much as we will mean to her," Rhonda says, "We can't tell her just yet, but someday our daughter will learn that no one could have been more important in all our lives than our friend, her Aunt Julie."

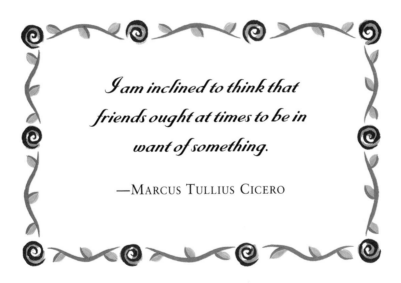

I am inclined to think that friends ought at times to be in want of something.

—Marcus Tullius Cicero

Love Thy Friend

As he drove home along the familiar roads to their house, Stuart wondered how he'd broach the subject with Mary. And in the end, he knew he'd do what he always did with Mary. He'd just up and tell the truth.

So, when he walked through the door and saw Mary, he said quickly, "I have a surprise for you. June's son Philip is going to call."

Mary looked perplexed for a moment. "Why not June herself?"

"I don't know," he answered.

"Stuart, it's been more than thirty years since I've heard a word. Is she—well, is she still alive?"

"All I know is that Philip called me to ask for our home phone number, and he said you'd hear from him. I guess you'll just have to wait."

"I've been waiting all these years," Mary mused, half to herself, half to Stuart. "It's been so awful never knowing what happened to her. There we were, best friends in high school. You remember, that's why she was maid of honor at our wedding. And then I was matron of honor when she married poor Harry."

"I liked him, too," Stuart reminded her. "Too bad. He died so young, leaving her with those three kids. Didn't you used to see her after Harry died?"

"I not only saw her, but after she moved away I sent birthday cards and mailed her letters. Then, after a few years, there was nothing. I never stopped sending cards and letters, but when they came back with those post office stamps saying 'Address Unknown,' even you urged me to stop sending letters."

"Face it. Address Unknown doesn't sound promising."

"But Philip called you, and—listen! There's the phone."

Stuart picked up the telephone. "It's Philip. It's for you."

She took the phone slowly. "Philip?"

"Aunt Mary—"

She smiled. He must be in his mid-thirties, and he still called her Aunt Mary.

"Your mother?" she began.

Philip told his story quickly and without emotion. After his dad died, the family moved a few towns away. They didn't have much money, and his mom had to take a job cleaning office buildings. June, a proud woman, didn't want anyone to feel sorry for her in her reduced circumstances, so she stopped communicating with all her school friends. Later it seemed awkward to renew relationships. Then, two years ago, June remarried and told her husband about her friend Mary. He urged her to call so he might meet Mary and her family. Finally she was going to pick up the dropped stitches of her oldest and dearest friendship. The week she planned to call, she had a stroke. "She was in a coma for months, and no one expected her to live," Philip explained. "But she did live, and even though doctors thought she'd never walk, she does with help. The thing is that Mom can't talk or write. She's only about an hour's drive from here, and she and her husband have a nice little house. The other day I mentioned your name to see how she'd react, and I could tell that she wanted to see you. Will you come?"

The next day Mary loaded her car with photo albums of June's girlhood, of both their weddings and their babies and drove to visit her old friend. Mary was so nervous that she stopped twice for coffee. But once Mary arrived at June's house, she walked up the steps, put a smile on her face, opened the door, took one look at her childhood friend, and it was if they'd never been apart. They hugged. They kissed. And they cried. Oh, how they cried.

And then June, June who had not spoken a word since her stroke, took her friend's face in her hands. "M-M-M-Mary," she half-said.

Mary put her arms around her friend and held her close.

"Stuart," Mary told her husband later, "when she said my name, we all knew that we were seeing a miracle of love. We were all crying, but the thing you could actually see was the love in that room. Everybody felt it. June's sons knew what we meant to one another. Her husband sensed it, too. And June and me? Well, we both know that nothing can be the same with us, but you see, we still have this real love from the heart. Oh, I know we can't talk together the way we once did. But friends, old friends, don't need to say a word to recognize that kind of love. What happened to her doesn't change the way we love one another. From now on I'll be going back to see June often."

Love thy friend, and be faithful unto him....

—ECCLESIASTICUS 27:17

Time and Space

The little Indiana airport had been snowbound for several hours, and now the clouds were lifting. Flights were coming in, and Diane knew planes would soon be taking off. And she would be on one of them.

How hard it had been to come home when the old home was no longer her real home.

But there had been a time when this was home. A time when she and Penny had been best friends. Improbable as it seemed, she and Penny had not seen one another for almost ten years. They'd both left Indiana for college, then continued in different directions, one north and one south. Still, she thought about Penny more than any other friend.

Coming home to Indiana always made her memories of Penny come to life. Penny, who'd known Diane's parents as long as she and who listened patiently whenever Diane appreciated or depreciated them, sometimes in the same sentence. Penny, whose older brother had always teased thirteen-year-old Diane about her tiny bosom.

Last year, when Diane came home to bury her father, she learned Penny's mother had died the year before. She'd written to Penny at once, a letter full of memories of both their parents. And Penny had responded quickly from Florida, where she now lived, a loving letter telling of her children, her husband, her life.

Now, as Diane looked across the snowy airfield, she thought of Penny. She thought of mittens and snowsuits and other snowy, sunny days. She turned back to talk to her brother when—

Impossible! Unbelievable! But it was—

It was Penny. Standing at the next gate was Penny! Penny, who still looked—oh wonder of wonders—she still looked like Penny. Older, but still that sweet, dear face. Oh, Penny.

At that moment Penny blinked in disbelief. The two ran toward each other. They held each other tightly and then stepped back, frozen in memory, each to look at the girl she remembered and the woman she now saw. Penny looked at

Diane with a love born of winter nights and homework, giggles and girl secrets.

Diane was so full of love and joy that she could not speak.

And then in an instant, at the very same moment, the two women broke the silence. They became girls again, and just as their childhood had been lived in harmony, now together they asked, "Remember the Hill?"

The Hill? In winter it was called the Hill; in summer the Swamp. But regardless of its name, it was the place they played. Without saying a word they knew they both remembered begging their dads to give them the wooden doors from back porches, doors they'd pretend were big sleds as they went sliding down the snowy Hill. Come summertime, the Hill turned into a place parents called the smelly old swamp. None of them could imagine what their kids were doing out there. But it wasn't smelly. It was the Hill. You had to be a kid to understand. It was special. Summer or winter, it was theirs.

"I remember," Diane answered. "I remember it all."

And, with a love of shared times and shared friends, a love of parents who were no more, a love of a place they'd once called home, a love that went so far beyond words, Penny put her arms around Diane. Then gently, very gently, she patted her old friend on the back.

Not a word was spoken, but Diane heard it all.

Diane heard the heartache of Penny's first marriage—the one to the classmate Diane never had liked. She heard the sweetness of joys remembered and sadness forgotten. She heard the satisfaction of watching children grow, and she heard the happiness in rediscovering a time one sometimes forgets but never loses.

Indeed, Diane was listening so hard to the unspoken she scarcely heard her plane called.

Finally her brother tugged at her sleeve. "It's time to go," he whispered.

"I don't know how we will do it, but we will see one another," Diane said as she pulled from the embrace.

"Yes, we will," Penny answered. "I want this moment again."

Time and space are only forms of thought.

—EDITH NESBIT, *THE STORY OF THE AMULET*

A Passion for Friends

Maybe it was because I was an only child. Or it may have been because her friends mattered so much to her that my mother always wanted to be certain that I had friends.

Indeed she was so concerned about friendships for me that she even gave me my first best friend.

My friend's name was Marilyn, and she was Edith's daughter. Edith was my mother's best friend.

Marilyn and I called each other's mother "Aunt," pretended we were the sisters neither of us had, and for the first ten years of our lives did everything together, as did our mothers.

When our mothers learned to crochet, we had matching sweater coats (mine was navy; Marilyn's, brown). With our mothers we went downtown to lunch in department store tearooms, saw countless movies (*Sleeping Beauty* was our favorite), played for hours in Marilyn's playhouse—a converted gardener's cottage behind the main house—or went up to the third floor of our house because that was where the dolls and dress-up clothes were kept.

We knew one another's grandparents and aunts, had sleepovers almost weekly, and told each other secrets too good for mothers to know. The few half-truths about sex that we learned from books and other kids we kept to ourselves. Convinced that no one was as much fun as we were, we suffered our real cousins and the children of our mothers' friends with measured moans. Or was it fear that another little girl might come between us and spoil our perfect friendship?

And then Marilyn and her family moved, and while our friendship continued, it was never quite the same. I found other best friends in my new junior high, but now I was a teenager, so the girls didn't play with dolls or act out the imagined lives of others the way Marilyn and I did. It was many years before I understood how our play world had allayed my childhood fears.

The years went by, and with them came new life stages called marriage, children, divorce, illness, widowhood—yet even as the mileposts changed, the route to self-discovery was unchanged.

I talked to friends and found myself.

Along the way I have forged new friendships; each of them relates to and understands some part of me. In each of them is a germ of my first best friend, Marilyn.

No matter how my life changes, my need for friends continues.

Over the years I have had occasional meetings with Marilyn. And when we find one another either by choice or chance, we embrace in a mist of memory. We shed tears for lost parents and lost years, and for a moment we each move back into the old, safe neighborhood called innocence, the little neighborhood that prepared us for the bigger world.

All people have their fancies . . .
but I have a passion for friends. . . .

—PLATO

The Seasons of Friendship

MEMORABLE FRIENDS

Memory is what
We choose to remember
And friends are those
Who want to remember
The very same things.

Time and Seasons

It was midnight, and my friend Phyllis, who had come to visit for the weekend, was having a cozy chat with me. I was curled in a chair next to the fireplace, and she was relaxing on the sofa. Suddenly Phyllis stood and said, "Let's rearrange the furniture."

I think the male equivalent of those words is, "Let's play football."

So, at 1 A.M., a time when respectable women like us should have been long abed, we were still pushing furniture and grunting like two stevedores.

By 3 A.M. we'd finished. "You know what the room needed, don't you?" Phyllis asked.

Me? I didn't even know there was anything wrong with the room in the first place. I thought I was just being an accommodating hostess and letting her regroup my chairs. "No," I mumbled, "what did the room need?"

"A circle," she said slowly and distinctly. "Every room must have its own sewing circle. The chairs and sofa and little pull-up chairs must be in a perfect circle so everyone can talk together. You see, you had two conversational groupings. It's all right, but, well, I must tell you that it's just not as good as a sewing circle."

Next morning I thought the room looked pretty good, and so it still remains. I've noticed that ever since the furniture was moved people stay longer and talk more. I like that.

I thought about Phyllis and her sewing circle when daughter Kathy and her family went to Cleveland to visit brother Rob and his family. "About one A.M. Denise and I were sitting in the family room talking," Kathy recalled, "and all of a sudden I said to her, 'Let's move the furniture. That sofa should be here, and that table should be there.' So we did."

Next time I visited Rob and Denise, I realized that what Kathy and Denise had done, knowingly or by instinct, was to create a sewing circle.

Is there something in our genes that makes us women gravitate to the idea of the sewing circle and the quilting bee?

Does friendship have its circles, its seasons, its times and its reasons?

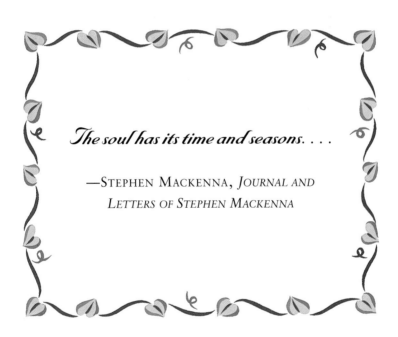

The soul has its time and seasons. . . .

—STEPHEN MACKENNA, *JOURNAL AND LETTERS OF STEPHEN MACKENNA*

THE DARKNESS OF MY FRIEND

She died today. My friend died.
I don't know how.
It doesn't really matter.
I know she was tortured by a blackness
She never could make people understand.

She tried to make me understand.
"They call it depression. It doesn't deserve
  a name that good.
"There is a blackness, and I go headfirst
  into that black.
"I can't get out. I can't get out.
"Some people tell me I don't really have
  to be like this.

*"Can't they understand I don't want to
be like this?"*

*In the black world where she struggled
Were we, her strong, sure friends,
Too weak to help?
Were we so blinded by the glare and light
of our own lives
We were afraid to look into her blackness
Lest it darken our bright days?*

*She died today. My friend died.
And this evening
In my shadow was a reflection of
The darkness of my friend.*

At the Loss of a Friend

When my friend Liz was wid-owed, I went to my desk as I have so many times in search of the words that I might write, words to assuage a friend's loss.

I cannot offer trite phrases. It's getting late in the day, the time for truth. My mother, who was twice widowed, told me after her first widowhood that it never gets better; it just gets ordinary.

It never did get ordinary for me. It has never seemed everyday to me to be a widow; it feels out of step. I've always been an independent woman, but widowhood is such an unspeakable loss that the space left is shockingly vast.

To be totally honest, I will have to tell Liz that although families are wonderful, thoughtful, and helpful, it is not family who will fill her days and warm her nights. Although her children may indeed be dear, sweet, and loving, one's children are just that—children. And children can do only so much for parents. When it comes right down to everyday living, like putting one foot in front of the other and facing dishes in the sink and mail on the desk—only one thing can keep you going: friends.

I know that Liz's friends were on call when her husband became ill. Friends were there through the terrible times. And I'm sure she has a houseful now. But the ones who are still there after the last casserole disappears are the stayers; the others are the goers, off to the next event. Staying is what separates acquaintances from friends.

"So, Liz, I guess what I really want to tell you is that this is a time to make sure you let your friends into your life.

"With every loss, each of us must open all lines to our friends, because it is friends who keep us going when we can't figure why we ought to keep going. It is friends who knock at the door, call on the phone, and give a reason to get up each morning—because a job and a family just aren't reason enough.

"Losing a partner never becomes an old story. Whether it's by death or divorce makes no difference. When a woman loses a man, a part of her dies, too.

"The empty place has a name. It is called 'I still miss him.'

There's a danger in widowhood. We can replay the daily doses of his love and attention in a memory machine, but if we do it too long and too often, memory can become a substitute for life.

"Friends will make sure that doesn't happen. Only friends can schedule and plan a survivor's reemergence back into the world.

"There are no guarantees that happiness follows when a woman loves a man.

"But when a woman declares herself a friend, and her friendship is returned, that's practically an ironclad lifetime commitment.

"You have been that kind of lifetime friend, Liz.

"And that's why friends will always be waiting for you. Don't be afraid to make the first call. Don't be afraid to extend invitations. Keep your home and your heart open, and let your friends fill both.

"I send you my love and my prayers for your continuing courage in a to-be-continued life. . . ."

The deep grief we feel at the loss of a friend arises from the feeling that in every individual there is something which no words can express. . . .

—SCHOPENHAUER

Some Little Kindness

Adrienne was one of those women who was part of a longtime marriage that ran out of steam around the second decade. When the marriage ended, Adrienne decided to put a whole new spin on life and go to a place where she had no history.

She made up her mind to move to San Francisco.

She knew it would not be easy to seek new ties, but she had spent several years traveling to San Francisco as part of her job in international banking, had a few work acquaintances and knew some nice women there, so she knew she could make herself comfortable—at least in the beginning. She considered herself emotionally prepared for the move to the city.

But now she was entering her sixth month of life as a San Francisco single woman, and it was tough. Damned tough.

Everybody knew more people than she did.

It seemed everybody knew more everything than she did.

No one had ever told her how much San Francisco loved its natives, that it would take time to belong.

As she looked around, she felt sure everybody belonged— except her. She was on the outside, her nose pressed up against the bakery window.

However, quite by accident, she had met a nice man in the elevator of her apartment house. His name was Glen. He was in his mid-fifties, probably three or four years her senior. It wasn't a romance, but that was okay. She wasn't ready for love. Not yet anyway. Would it ever be more than it was now? Who knew? She was fumbling and stumbling her way with him; she couldn't elevate their alliance to the term "relationship." She called it a friendship set to dating.

One day Glen called at her office and invited her to go a charity ball.

I've arrived, she thought. I'm going to be a real San Francisco woman. It took her the two days to quiet the butterflies. She bought a new dress, and had her hair done (two things she almost never did before any event). Adrienne prided herself on the fact that if it wasn't already in her closet, it was proof that she didn't really need it. Further, she was convinced that no woman with any sense of responsibility or social conscience should ever buy a dress for a single occasion (wedding dresses excepted).

But, as she looked in the mirror the night of the party, Adrienne gave herself a passing grade. This is as good as I get, she thought. Still, she worried. Who will I know? Who will talk to me? The waiters will know more people than I.

Struggling through the cocktail hour with a smile pasted where her mouth used to be, she knew her worst fears were coming true. She didn't know anyone; no one spoke to her, and Glen seemed as much an outsider as she.

Glen and Adrienne sipped their drinks and smiled wanly at one another.

Would dinner never be announced?

Finally she took her placecarded seat at the table. Glen was next to her. She breathed a small sigh of relief because the man on the other side of her was obviously so dazzled by his dinner companion that he never even turned to her to introduce himself.

Across from her was a distinguished-looking couple. The

woman seemed to be looking at Adrienne, but she wasn't certain. Then, after a few minutes, the woman smiled at Adrienne. Adrienne looked over her shoulder. There was no one behind her. Could this woman be smiling at Adrienne Nobody?

Yes. She was smiling at her. And now, wonder of wonders, the woman got up from her chair, came around the table and extended her arms. "Adrienne," she said, "I'm Paula King, the twins' sister."

Of course. Now she could put it together. The twins had grown up with Adrienne. They'd all known one another since they were five years old. Paula—so this was Paula! The glamorous sister the twins adored, the sister who went to California to live. Now here she was, and Adrienne was meeting her.

"Erica told me you were coming here to live, so I've been looking for you," she said.

Adrienne was dizzy with delight.

She turned to Glen and explained that Paula had been away at school as a young girl; they'd never known one another, but still each knew of the other.

"Welcome to San Francisco," Paula said aloud. And then she whispered, "I'm going to call you tomorrow. You know, I have no little sister here, and I miss not having one."

A few years later Adrienne was talking to Paula. "You know, I keep thinking how you've changed my life here, what a wonderful time I've had. What if I'd never gone to that dinner? What if we hadn't met? Who would have let me be a sister?"

"Probably someone else," Paula said. "You know, little sister, I feel lucky, too."

"The thing about this is that there's no way I can pay you back."

"Only one way." Paula smiled. "Go out and find a little sister for yourself. But don't look for a big sister. You already have one."

My liking always wants
some little kindness
to kindle it.

—GEORGE ELIOT, *MIDDLEMARCH*

Things You Don't Want to Tell

Janine checked her coat, and when she spotted Frannie at the corner table, she walked quickly toward her.

"So what's the good news?" Frannie asked even before Janine could sit down.

"How can you tell there's good news?" Janine said, laughing.

"Because when a woman glows the way you do, she's either just had a facial or found a new boyfriend. Which is it?"

"New man."

"Details, please."

"You are not going to believe this one."

"Try me."

"He is absolutely divine. He is the smartest, most attractive, most interesting man I ever met. He's fun to be with, and he cares so much for me. He is so good to me. He can't do enough for me. I stayed home from work the other day because I had a cold, and he said it was so lonely at the office without me that he came at noon with chicken soup he picked up at the deli, and—"

"Whoa. Did you say that he missed you at work?"

"Yes."

"Hmmmm. Romance in the workplace. No wonder you were out sick. Haven't you read any of those books that say office sex is bad for your health?"

"Oh, Frannie, I've never felt like this before."

"That's so good it sounds like the lyric to a forties song. However, let's order, and then you can tell me what's wrong with him, because I don't know if I can live in a world with someone that perfect. He must have one little fault, one teeny crack in the armor."

"There's just one glitch. But let's order first. I'll tell you in a minute."

They each glanced at the menu, but Frannie couldn't help herself. She had to steal another look at Janine. She'd never seen her friend so animated. This love was obviously causing the glow, and Frannie thought how happy she was for her. She knew Janine had taken care of an ailing mother, made peace with a difficult sister. It was about time she was rewarded by life.

They gave their orders quickly, and Frannie said, "So what's the problem? His mother hates you?"

"Worse." Now Janine lowered her eyes. "He's married."

"No!" Frannie wanted to pound the table. Married? How could an honorable man get involved with a woman as decent and kind as Janine?

"That's why I wanted to talk to you, Frannie. I need some advice in dealing with this. I figured you'd know what to do."

"Why did you think I'd know?"

"Because you're twenty years older and about twenty times smarter. You see, this is the best my life has ever been, and I don't want to mess things up."

"You're not messing things up. He is. He's the one who's married. You're not."

"But it's not a true marriage. He and his wife haven't really been married for ten years. Well, they're legally married, but it's not a loving relationship like ours." Janine looked across the table at her friend. "He says he's always been waiting for a woman like me, but this just isn't the right time to leave home because he's due for a big promotion, and he wouldn't be able to deal with a divorce and a new job at the same time, and—"

"—and he wants things to go on just as they are for a while," Frannie said, finishing her sentence.

"How did you know what he said?"

"Because a long time ago someone said those same words to me. Once I was sitting where you are, and a woman I liked a lot was sitting in this chair. I didn't ask her advice. She called me and said she wanted to meet me for lunch because she worked with me, and she could see that I was getting very deeply involved with a man destined to be the next president of the company."

"And he was married?"

"Yes."

"So what happened?"

"I asked her how the story might have a happy ending."

"Did she tell you?"

"Yes." Frannie sighed. "She told me that my story could never have a happy ending. She said that the only happy ending could have been written before anything started. She also gave me a line to use anytime a married man wanted to get a little too friendly. She said tell him, 'It has always been my belief that married men should fool around with married women and single men should fool around with single women. I'm single, and you're married, so get lost.'"

"Obviously, you didn't do that."

Frannie shook her head. "No, and I ended up with a broken heart. Because no matter how smart a woman is, there are times she will do foolish things. Falling in love with a married man is usually a foolish thing. I know that in your case it probably started out innocently enough, but along the way you lose your innocence. The reality of the unreality gets the better of you. But an affair isn't the same as a lifelong love. Affairs always look so good because there are no stopped-up sinks in an affair, just stopped-up lives. So my advice is, get out. And get out fast before you are really hurt by this man."

"That's not what I wanted you to say, Frannie."

"No, dear, I think it's just what you wanted to hear. You wanted someone to stop you before you really got burned, and you know deep down in your heart that you could never be happy if you thought you had broken up someone's home. You're so good and decent that you wanted somebody to wake you up and send you home while there is still time. I did it, but I didn't want to be the one to say these things."

Janine shook her head sadly, and her eyes filled with tears.

Frannie reached across the table and put her hand on top

of Janine's. "Oh, Janine, I'd give anything not to tell you this. Hurting a friend is no way to keep a friend, but if I weren't honest, would I be a friend?"

A friend can tell you things you don't want to tell yourself.

—Francis Ward Wheeler, *Boat Song*

More Than Friendship

When Carol died, hostesses all over town took out their Rolodexes so they might be the first to fix up Sherwin. Widower Sherwin, age forty-nine, was the hottest bachelor since Warren Beatty gave up the single life.

But Sherwin was a reluctant date. "I'm not ready," he said to the ladies who called. "Yes," he would answer patiently, "I am sure your friend is beautiful and talented, and she is probably also thrifty, brave, and reverent, but I'm not in the market. Not yet anyway."

Still the ladies called, and still Sherwin refused to go out. His turndown was always polite. Very polite.

Then, one night at a charity dinner, Sherwin was seated

next to Bunny, an old friend, a friend of his wife's and his, a woman who had been their hostess many times and who had been a guest in their home as well.

"How's it going, Sherwin?" she asked.

"I can be honest with you," he said. "I'm so sad that some nights I can't bear going home. My house is filled with memories of Carol. I have to sell that house."

"Oh, really?" asked Bunny. "Sell the house and uproot your life right now? Let me ask you something. Is the house totally to your liking?"

"Yes and no," Sherwin replied. "It's the right size and a good location, but it's her house. It's just the way she wanted it."

Bunny took a deep breath and asked, "Sherwin, are you telling me that maybe it's not exactly the way you'd want it?"

"That's right," he admitted. "It's not exactly what I want. You see, Carol took the library and turned it into a TV room, and I don't have a place for my books and papers. And the bedroom is kind of frilly. . . ."

Bunny nodded. "I know what you mean. Remember—I've been married, too, and we all make accommodations for a spouse's tastes. I suggest you just take that TV room and turn it into your own library. Put your desk in there. Get yourself a fax machine or whatever you need. And about that bedroom . . . call a decorator or the furniture store, and get yourself a new bed. Repaper and paint. Sherwin, you don't need a new house. You just need to make the old house your house."

Months later Sherwin saw Bunny again. "Thanks for giving me my house," he said. "You're the first person who didn't think that being a friend and helping me fix my life meant introducing me to a new woman."

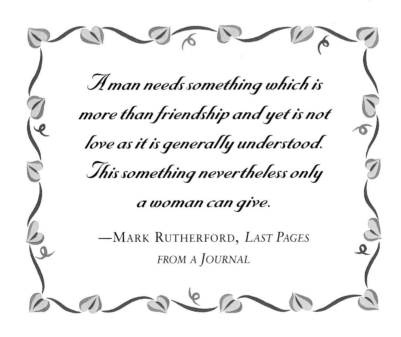

A man needs something which is more than friendship and yet is not love as it is generally understood. This something nevertheless only a woman can give.

—MARK RUTHERFORD, *LAST PAGES FROM A JOURNAL*

TITLES

Sometimes it is a slender thread,
Sometimes a strong, stout rope;
She clings to one end,
I the other;
She calls it friendship;
I call it hope.

Choosing Our Friends

In the 1930s and 1940s Hollywood was the mecca for kids from Oklahoma—and practically everyplace else. Hollywood was where dreams came true, and every girl worth her subscription to a movie magazine knew that the drugstore at Hollywood and Vine was where she could stop for a soda and end up a star.

Full of optimism, teenage Grace came from Oklahoma. Unlike most of the kids in Hollywood, however, Grace wasn't there to pursue a wild dream. She was there to lead a sensible life; it just happened that she was the cousin of a famous movie star, and Aunt Dora, the star's mother, had offered to take her in when Grace's mother fell ill.

Both aunt and cousin could not have been sweeter or kinder to Grace. Whenever the famous star/cousin went to a party, she took Little Cousin. Grace knew that back in Oklahoma they'd probably think that going to parties with Clark Gable and Tyrone Power was really swell. But Grace was more frightened than thrilled at the collections of famous guests who always looked around the room as if they needed to find someone more important.

Still, she could not stop hoping, so each time Big Cousin took her to a party, Grace would close her eyes and say to herself, "Maybe tonight I will find a friend."

But each time she stayed meekly in a corner, afraid to venture forth, too timid to speak.

And then one night at a party Grace saw a young woman her age, a creature of such extraordinary beauty that Grace blinked in astonishment. Surprisingly, like Grace, she was standing alone. Despite her remarkable beauty, she was at the fringe, looking at the party from the outside.

"And that was the moment I realized that people are people," Grace recalls. "I knew this wasn't Oklahoma, but instinctively I knew I could talk to this woman because even though she was prettier than I, she looked just as lonely. I thought about what I might say to her, and then I realized that she had the most extraordinary way of making up her eyes, so I went up to her and said, 'Pardon me, but would you tell me how you put on your mascara? I never saw anything like it.'"

The young woman smiled and said, "Oh, let me tell you. But before I do, who are you, and why are you here?"

And so Grace told her about Famous Cousin and Aunt Dora, and she told her about Oklahoma and being in Hollywood as a relative, not a star.

And the young woman, although a well-known actress, confessed that she went to these parties without ever talking to anyone, never knowing who would talk to her. "I don't have any friends," she said quietly.

"I don't have any friends either," Grace echoed.

And as the two frightened outsiders spoke, each knew she would never have to say those words again.

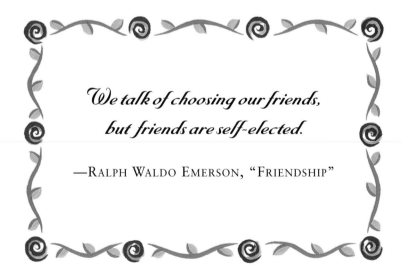

We talk of choosing our friends,
but friends are self-elected.

—RALPH WALDO EMERSON, "FRIENDSHIP"

The Soul

You have to know this one thing about girls. When you're a teenage girl, what you want even before you want a boyfriend is a girl who's a best friend. You need someone for that whisper-in-the-dark, I-have-a-secret relationship. Manya was that kind of friend for me.

"We met in the seventh grade and had what I thought was a really affectionate friendship, but there was something strange. As we got older, I started feeling tense with her. I couldn't explain it, but it seemed there was a wall between us, a Lucite wall I called it. It wasn't a glass wall, because I could have shattered that. This was a wall I could never break down. I used to wonder why she kept her distance and what I was doing wrong.

"Then, when we were in high school, I had a huge crush on a boy on the football team. I thought he was so cute and asked her if she didn't think so, too.

"She said no, and when I looked surprised, she finally got up the courage to tell me she was a lesbian.

"In some ways it affected our friendship, and in other ways it didn't. I never again felt comfortable telling her about crushes and dates and things like that, but even though I couldn't talk to her the way I talked to the other girls, she'd made me feel close and special because she had told me her secret. And once I knew she was the one putting that distance between us, I guess I was relieved, because I got rid of any guilt. I figured I wasn't the one causing the barrier in our friendship. You know, when you're a teenager you always think you must have done something wrong if girls you like don't respond strongly to you. This taught me not to blame myself for everything.

"When I went to college it just happened that I was assigned a lesbian roommate, and I think we were able to become close friends because I already had a lesbian friend. I wasn't threatened by her sexual preference.

"I still maintain contact and feel close to both of these women, even though each leads an openly gay life and I am married and have children.

"Long ago each of these women made romantic overtures to me. I told them both no, and that was it. But the truth is that I was flattered and pleased that they wanted me. I guess I would have been disappointed if they hadn't. I took it as a real proof of the love of each of them."

—*A Connecticut Housewife*

You cannot hide the soul.

—Herman Melville,
Moby-Dick

Wandering

Hannah opened the locked drawer in her dresser.

It had been years since she had locked the drawer. What could be in it? Who could remember?

Surprise! The drawer slid open easily, and there was nothing in it. Then why had she locked it in the first place? Wait. There in the corner. Two pieces of crystal. Hannah picked them up and turned them over in her hand. And as she did she puzzled over them trying to remember why—why these had been saved—and in a locked drawer.

Why had she kept these pieces of rock that looked like slivers from a glacier?

And then, as if awakening from a dream, she remembered that terrible time she had worked so hard to forget. . . .

. . . Seven years ago, in the dead of winter, the doctors, the white-coated doctors, had told Hannah that in a few months Karl would be dead.

Dead.

Dead as this winter of disillusion.

Dead as their once-young dreams.

When she left the hospital that night, the city was frosted with a layer of crystal ice. Slick, slippery ice on the city sidewalks, the sidewalks he would never walk again.

I can't give in, she promised herself.

I will keep hope alive.

Next week we'll go here. . . .

Next month we'll go there. . . .

Each day she visited Karl in the hospital, and she promised him life. At first he was eager to accept her gift.

But as the weeks and months wore on, Karl was no stronger. When at last she brought him home, and they both faced the weakness and the frailty that was Karl, the last traces of her optimism seemed to fade. Finally even Hannah was ready to believe that there wasn't going to be a next month or a next year.

But she could not give up everything. Now she held fast to each day. Hannah would wake up, look out the window, and say, "Well, it's Thursday and we're still here. So how about that!"

Some of her old best friends did not appreciate her myopic vision of the world. Insane optimism, one called it. But there was a young art director at the magazine where she worked, and over shared sandwiches and cups of coffee, she had confided to him things she found she couldn't say now to all her old friends. Perhaps it was because he was young and life stretched ahead of him; perhaps that was why he could listen to her and nod in agreement when she tried to hold on to each day and avoid contemplating her tomorrows.

One morning the young man walked into her office and said, "Do you know that crystals have healing power?"

She shook her head. "No, but tell me about them. Please. Tell me now."

"There's really nothing to tell. I will give you these crystals," he said quietly. "Just keep rubbing them, and remember they are from a friend who cares. Remember that the love of friends keeps you alive."

"Will they keep my husband alive?"

"Try," he said.

Hannah shook her head. How could crystals make her husband live after the doctors had given up?

But she took them home to show Karl, and as she stood at the side of the bed with the crystals in her hand, she saw that she was holding them in such a way that they caught the north light coming through the window.

Hannah smiled. Pretty. So pretty. But that sweet, foolish young man. How could he think these crystals might keep Karl alive?

"Karl, do you see the light?" she whispered.

"Yes, but that's just the tip of the iceberg," Karl said.

Hannah nodded, because she knew there was something profound in Karl's words. The light was but a part of their love, the part the world could see. Could the friendship in that young man's heart have matched the love in theirs?

"Touch the crystals again," she urged Karl. "They are us."

"Then come lie beside me," he said, "and don't cry. Promise not to cry crystal tears."

And so Hannah lay beside him. They held one another, and he dried her tears.

Even months after the funeral, her tears would stop when she looked at the crystals and thought of the northern lights and the fire of love.

. . . And now, seven years later on a hot summer day she had opened that locked drawer by accident.

But there were no accidents in life, were there?

No, this is an omen, she thought. A sign from Karl. Our love still shines in the crevices of the crystal in my hand.

Her eyes filled, and her body was tense with anticipation as she rolled the crystals in her hand. She held the crystals up to the lamp on the chest and waited. But there was nothing.

Where had all the lights gone? It was as if she held two pieces of unpolished stone.

She turned the crystals this way and that. Again she waited. She moved closer to the window, held the crystals to the strong sun and waited.

But no matter how she tried to shape the truths she held in her hand, she could not see the northern lights and the fire of love.

That was when Hannah let the tears come.

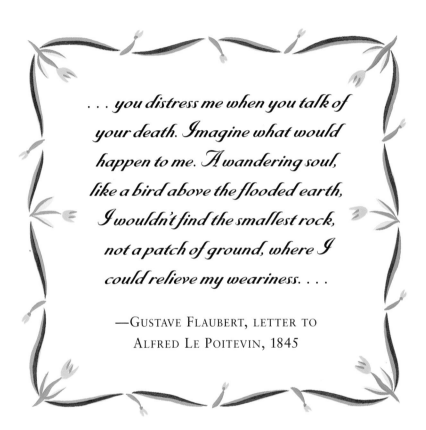

. . . *you distress me when you talk of your death. Imagine what would happen to me. A wandering soul, like a bird above the flooded earth, I wouldn't find the smallest rock, not a patch of ground, where I could relieve my weariness.* . . .

—GUSTAVE FLAUBERT, LETTER TO
ALFRED LE POITEVIN, 1845

Nothing I Would Not Do

From the time she was six or seven Lucia had had a fantasy of a big double bed where she and her husband—her handsome, loving husband—would live their lives. On this bed their babies would be born. On this bed their children would cuddle while snow drifted outside. And on this bed, when she was very old, her life would end.

When Lucia met Barney, she figured her dream was about to come true. What she saw delighted her; he was handsome and rich and so smitten with Lucia that he bought her a four-carat diamond and a three-bedroom house. And Lucia was so enamored of Barney that her eyes and heart would not let her hear what her friends and family tried to tell her.

Too self-centered, one of Lucia's old boyfriends said.

Too old for you, her mother said.

Too irresponsible, her father said.

Too interested in other women, her brother warned.

But Lucia was twenty-two, and she knew what she wanted.

By the time she was twenty-seven she had learned what the others had already known.

It was true, all true. Barney was too self-centered, too old, too irresponsible—and much too interested in other women.

But what is a wife to do?

Lucia, after five years of marriage, had not only her husband to consider but also three infant daughters. And Lucia knew what it meant to grow up in a divided house; her parents had divorced when she was three, and she had sworn through all the years of her childhood that she would never make a child of hers live through years of split loyalties as she had.

Lucia tried to get family counseling; she tried to persuade Barney to see a psychologist, a psychiatrist, even an astrologer; she pleaded in shrill desperation—but his answer to her appeals was to find more reasons to stay away from his home.

Yet, sad as Lucia was, she could not bring herself to talk about the problems with anyone. Not even Michelle.

Michelle had been delighted when Lucia and Barney moved next door, and even more pleased when Lucia's first baby arrived at the same time as Michelle's third. "It's terrific for all of us," Michelle assured her husband. "The babies will play together, and all of us parents will have a good time together, too."

The first time that Michelle invited Lucia and Barney for dinner with the children, Lucia and the children came. "Barney's working late," Lucia explained.

No one questioned it.

But when Barney repeatedly failed to show up for planned dinners at his home, Lucia stopped explaining.

"Please stop planning things with Lucia and Barney; it's too awkward," Michelle's husband protested. "He's just a bad guy."

"But he's Lucia's bad guy, and she wants him," Michelle reminded him.

"Then see Lucia alone, and leave the husbands out of it," he said.

So the friendship became a wife-to-wife thing instead of a family relationship.

One afternoon Lucia stopped by to see Michelle. When she walked into the familiar blue-and-white kitchen, she was surprised and pleased to find Bill Barrows, a man she hadn't seen in ten years.

"Bill. Bill Barrows," she repeated as if to assure herself he was real, not just a memory. "What are you doing at Michelle's—oh, I didn't m-m-mean that," she stammered.

"Bill's my cousin," Michelle said. "Didn't you know that?"

Lucia shook her head.

"How do you two know each other?" Bill asked.

"Neighbors," Lucia said easily.

"Lucia was my first girlfriend," Bill said, laughing. "I'll bet I haven't seen you for ten years . . ."

". . . ten years and three months," she interrupted. "That's when we were graduated from high school . . ."

". . . but you're as beautiful as you were in school."

Lucia blushed.

"And you still blush. Nobody blushes anymore, Lucia," he teased.

"Well, you should see her three daughters," Michelle told him. "They're beautiful, too."

"I'd like to. Will you and your husband invite me to see them?"

"Stop by before you leave," Lucia said.

"Careful," he warned, "or I may just scoop you all up and take you home. I'm still not married, Lucia. Never found another one like you."

"Oh, don't be silly," Lucia said. But even as she said the words, her heart did a little skip. What fun to have a man make a fuss over her!

Bill was still at Lucia's when Barney came home. "I just stopped by to pick up some papers for a meeting tonight," Barney called as he ran toward the stairs.

"Come meet my guest," Lucia said.

"No time," he answered, "but tell Michelle I said hi."

"It's not Michelle."

"Oh well, tell the girls hello from Daddy. I'll be home around midnight."

Bill looked at Lucia. "Does he do this often?"

"Well, he's really busy. You know his work is so intense, and—"

"—and his beautiful wife doesn't complain. You're one in a million, Lucia."

At breakfast the next morning Lucia asked, "And how was your meeting last night?"

"Good. Very good," Barney said. "But we didn't quite finish. I won't be home tonight."

"That's okay. I won't be home tonight either," Lucia said quietly.

"What do you mean you won't be home tonight?" Barney asked.

"I'm seeing an old friend."

"One of the girls from the neighborhood."

"One of the boys from my past. An old boyfriend."

"You can't go out with an old boyfriend."

"Why?"

"Because you're married."

"Oh, come on, Barney. You're married, and you're not going to be home."

"What's his name?"

"Bill," she said. "Bill Barrows."

"Bill Barrows? You mean William C. Barrows, the guy who just put the deal together for—"

"Yes."

"I didn't know you knew him."

"Maybe you ought to talk to me more. I know a lot of interesting people."

∽

Two weeks later Lucia called Michelle. "I owe you the best lunch in town. What about today?"

"Perfect," her friend answered.

And over a glass of white wine, Lucia confessed that she'd been miserable, upset, and unhappy—and then Bill Barrows came back into her life. "The crazy thing is that I have absolutely no romantic interest in Bill, not anymore. He belongs to another part of my life, and while it's comforting when an old friend is there again—no, I take it back—it's more than comfort. His presence has given me back a kind of confidence I'd lost. It's the strangest thing about Barney. I'd been suspicious about his activities for a long time, but I had too much at risk to complain. Now suddenly he has seen that another man finds me attractive, and he's worried that I will not be there for him. He told me he's been a fool, and he asked my forgiveness. Oh, he didn't say he had been seeing any other women. He just apologized for forgetting to put me first. Imagine. He's talking about things like reordering life priorities. I never thought I'd see the day. And it all happened without my making a big deal about it. Very quietly, with no speeches or ultimatums from me, Barney finds that he can do a lot of his work at home, and he doesn't seem to have nighttime meetings the way he used to. He tells me I look pretty, and the best part is that he's paying attention to the children. And guess what? He's finding that it's fun to be a father."

"I guess all that Barney needed was a wake-up call."

Lucia laughed. "But what's really so incredible is that if Bill hadn't just happened to visit you, and if he weren't your cousin—I'd still be so miserable."

"You never complained, but we are good enough friends that I could see how unhappy you were. I'm really glad you think things are changing for the better."

"Oh yes." Lucia smiled. "And there's nothing like a friend who helps—even when it's by chance."

Michelle was putting her baby down for a nap when the phone rang.

"Michelle," Bill Barrows said, "do you know what you've done?"

"Saved my friend's marriage," she said proudly.

"Look, honey," Bill said, "I didn't mind when you told me to pretend that I was your cousin so that I could see Lucia again. I didn't even mind that you got my name from her brother. I didn't mind that I was playing a game to help a woman get her husband to appreciate what he had. And I think you're a terrific friend to her. What I do mind, though, is I still really care for Lucia. Now what are you going to do, good friend?"

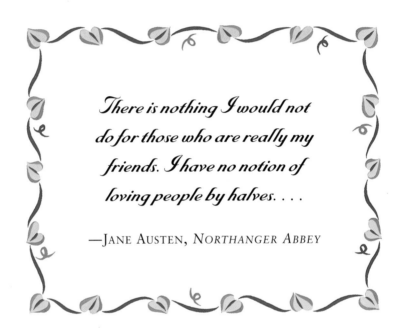

There is nothing I would not do for those who are really my friends. I have no notion of loving people by halves. . . .

—JANE AUSTEN, *NORTHANGER ABBEY*

The Relation of the Sexes

"So I'll ask you once again, Mom, what do you think? Should I go back to school or take the job in London?" Curtis's usually sunny smile was gone. Instead his brow was furrowed, and the corners of his mouth turned down. "Mom, it's the biggest decision of my life," he continued. "I don't know what to do."

Mona turned her wineglass slowly and looked across the restaurant table at her eldest son. She smiled, lost in memory of the times when her little boy acted willfully, without asking parental advice. Now that he was old enough to seek her advice, she was wise enough to be reluctant to give it. She sighed. "Your father and I have discussed this for days, dear, and we honestly don't know what to advise you. I told Dad just before he left on the trip to Tokyo that we were having dinner tonight, and I knew you wanted to reach some decision. He asked what I was going to tell you, and I said that my suggestion would be that you talk to Fritz. He agreed."

Curtis laughed. "I should have known."

"Meaning?"

"Meaning that I don't get it, Mom. I have two of the smartest parents, and whenever I have some kind of question, you tell me to talk to Fritz. Why?"

"Simple. He's my best friend."

"Mom, don't you think it's a little strange that you have a man as a best friend?"

"Oh, come on. How can you ask such a silly question?"

"Well, I'm not implying that you and Fritz have some kind of thing going on, but how does it happen that a woman—well, come on, Mom—how does a woman of your generation happen to have a man as a best friend?"

Mona took a deep breath. "Because, well, because. I guess you've been so busy being a male that you haven't found yet that friendship, my dear son, is not necessarily a same-sex relationship. I don't feel any need to explain myself to any of my children, but your question must mean that there's a lot you don't know about friendship."

"I didn't mean—"

"Hush a minute, Curtis. I'm going to tell you about a friendship that comes in four-part harmony. The first part is the relationship of two couples—Dad and me and Fritz and Marta. We all enjoy going to dinner or to concerts and plays and movies together.

"I have a friendship with Marta, too, and it's based a lot on our shared community interests.

"But the strongest friendship out of the relationship of our two families is mine with Fritz. He's my pal, my buddy. Fritz and I went to law school together, and we became good friends back in college. Each of us went on to marry someone we loved, someone each of us still loves. There was never any thought of romance between us, but somewhere between the books we studied and the cases we handled, a kind of trust and dependence on one another developed. I can talk to Fritz about my cases in a professional way, and I get clear-cut, professional advice because he knows my limitations, and he knows my beliefs and emotional climate. Conversely, the same is true. He consults me, but you only hear about the times I ask his advice."

"He's one of the smartest guys in town. And he asks your advice?"

"That's right."

"Then how come you can advise him but not me?"

"Maybe because I know he has enough seasoning to take my advice and combine it with his thoughts to reach a decision, and since I trust that combination, I want to see it work for you."

Curtis lifted his glass. "Okay, Mom. Here's to Fritz."

"No, let's make that toast to friendship. Because no matter what your decision is, I hope you're going to find a friend like Fritz who'll be there all your life."

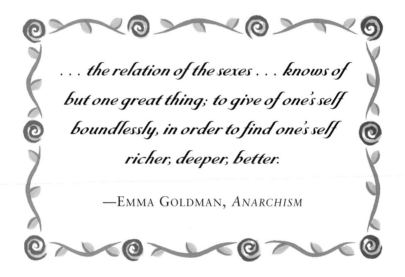

. . . the relation of the sexes . . . knows of but one great thing; to give of one's self boundlessly, in order to find one's self richer, deeper, better.

—EMMA GOLDMAN, *ANARCHISM*

According to Interests

Wendy sailed through the best waters of life, making friends in every port. Why not? She was beautiful, fun, and caring, a combination most people found irresistible. She was also generous in her friendships, assuming that those she liked would surely care for one another, so her numerous parties were always filled with those she thought should meet one another.

One day, when a New York friend came to Chicago, Wendy offered to have a small luncheon in her honor. The morning of the luncheon, just by chance, an English friend called to say she was in Chicago unexpectedly and wanted to say hello before returning to London. "Come join the luncheon," Wendy said blithely.

When New York friend met up with London friend, it was the beginning of a friendship that took on a life of its own. For the next several years, New York friend often stayed at the home of London friend, and London friend visited her new New York friend. Wendy, of course, maintained her separate friendships with both women.

Four years later Wendy called her New York friend to say she'd be in town for a day or two. "Oh, darling," cooed New York friend, "please come by. I'm going to have a small dinner party for my dear friend from London. You must meet her. You'll adore her."

"Excuse me," interrupted Wendy, "have you forgotten how you met her?"

"Oh," answered New York friend, "I can't remember any longer. I've known her forever."

"In that case," Wendy said, "I guess I've known her forever and a day because I'm the one who introduced you."

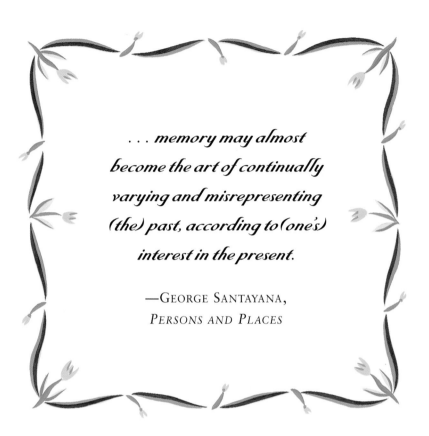

. . . *memory may almost become the art of continually varying and misrepresenting (the) past, according to (one's) interest in the present.*

—GEORGE SANTAYANA,
PERSONS AND PLACES

$\mathscr{R}ecess$

It is summer, and I am lying on the grass. I am not waiting for the kids on my block to play kick-the-can or jacks or jump rope. I'm more than half past childhood.

The friends on Clarendon Road long ago gave way to the friends on Edgerton Road, and now I don't think about the streets where friends live so much as I do the cities. I am so grown up now that I even have winter and summer friends. In the summer not only do I exchange heavy woolens for light cottons and linens, I switch from heavy-duty city friends to summer friends. Oh, they overlap at times—but there are changes.

Now it is more important to have a tennis partner than a theater friend. At the moment I have more in common with the woman who lives down the road and worries over Lyme disease and the deer problem with me than I do with my city-bound editor. And so I have come to think about the ways that place shapes us.

When I am in the city, I think little about my childhood and the friends whose songs still ring in my ears. But here in the country I get acute nostalgia and more than an occasional touch of suburban blues.

Although I am ordinarily a very private person, I find I talk more out here. I listen more, too. And I hear long-forgotten voices in the new ones. I read more. I retain more.

In her lovely book *The Making of a Writer,* Eudora Welty wrote, "Emotions do not grow old."

No, but we do. And sometimes we need the space and place to let our emotions catch up with us. Sometimes we even need to give our emotions a rest. Sometimes we have to forget about pleasing others and the need for conformity. Sometimes we just need to slow down and grow. Sometimes the best thing friends can do is to be good enough friends so that we don't need to see them or call them or remind them we love them.

Sometimes we just need friends to understand that we need aloneness right now. No, of course that doesn't mean that our love has stopped, but from time to time our need for love does take a recess.

The Quilting Bee Lives

KNOTS

Fear and habit
Keep us tied to our beginnings.
Only friends can untie
The complicated knots
To release us from
Our safe, warm beds
And let us venture forth
Unafraid
To experience life.

You Are Rich

The temperature must have been in the nineties, but Mary Jane shivered as she stood at the corner of Third Avenue and Seventy-ninth Street and dialed Liz's number.

"M.J., how are you?" Liz spoke quickly. You never knew when that crazy husband of M.J.'s would be picking up the phone.

"Okay. Now anyway."

"God, I wish you were here."

"I am."

"What?"

"I'm standing on your corner. I left him. My MG midget is packed to the gills with everything I could get in it."

"Did he hit you again?"

"Yes, but I'm all right. I mean I'm really all right, because I left and—hey, will you let me come up?"

Liz put the coffeepot on the stove. "Peter," she said to her boyfriend, "I know you'll understand, but M.J. came back to New York."

"That guy beat her up again?"

"Well, I know of two times she called the police, but her parents didn't want her to press charges. Too shameful, or something like that."

"At least she had the guts to leave," Peter said.

M.J. came into the apartment; her head was down and she almost shuffled. "I guess I'm back in New York for a while," she admitted shyly. "I think I was okay when I was here. Maybe I'm just not cut out to be a housewife."

"All I know is you can't be a beat-up housewife," Liz said. "Park your car, and bring your stuff here. This is where you're staying."

"I suppose you want to know exactly what happened," M.J. began.

"Listen, M.J., I don't want to know anything you don't feel like telling me. All I want is for you to be safe. You can stay with us."

"That's good of you," M.J. began, "but you guys need some privacy, and I can't—"

"Right. You can't go anywhere else," Liz said. "We're going to take care of you."

"How can you? I can't even take care of myself now. I don't know what to do first."

"Sure you do," Liz said. "First thing you'll do is clear everything from your car, then park it, and come back. And then tomorrow you'll start looking for a job."

M.J. nodded dutifully. Forty minutes later, and in an almost trancelike state, M.J. climbed the four flights and put everything she owned square in the middle of Liz's life.

For three months she read the newspaper ads, went on interviews, and slept on the sofa in Liz's living room.

The night Peter proposed to Liz, M.J. thought the living room seemed a touch too crowded. She told the couple she was going out for a beer.

"No way," said Peter. "You have to stay here while we get engaged. You're part of the deal."

M.J. had never felt more loved in her life. "Do you know what it means to leave an abusive man and come to this— this love?" she asked.

"No, but I can imagine," Liz said.

The first time M.J. got a job offer, she rushed home to tell Liz. "I'm going to take it," she said firmly. In the back of her mind M.J. could see fifteen hundred dollars and the freedom to find an apartment.

"You are not taking that job," Liz countered.

"I have to," M.J. insisted.

"It's not worthy of your talents," Liz said.

"I'm not even sure what my talents are," M.J. protested.

"I am," her friend answered. "You're smart and you're quick, and you are going to get a job that matches your abilities."

Liz kept her nightly pep talks going all through the next three months. She kept them going, even though M.J. was willing to wait tables, be a nanny, do anything to be independent.

"There's a big job out there for you, and we're here to see you get it," Liz told her.

"I'm going back for my fourth interview at McKinsey & Co.," M.J. told her one night. "But the problem is I don't have any more clothes. I've worn everything I have."

"We'll get you clothes," Liz said. "Between our friend Pat and me, you'll be the best-dressed job applicant in New York."

And the two, Liz and Pat, kept their wardrobes in circulation through the twelfth interview, the one that clinched the job.

It is fifteen years since that hot night on the corner of Third and Seventy-ninth. In those years M.J. has had a string of successful jobs, has put her life in order, and has made peace with her parents.

"I'm all right now only because of my friends," she admits easily. "I never looked back once I left that marriage, and Liz and Peter and Pat never forced me to do that. They were there with emotional support, with money—and believe me, that was back in the days when none of us had money, and the fifteen hundred dollars they lent me eventually for my own apartment were dollars they needed for themselves. They never took the superior attitude that people back home had; you know, the attitude that says that if your husband beat you, you must have deserved it. They trusted me when I didn't even trust myself. When I think about what they gave me, and I put it in words, I can say things like clothes and money and emotional support. But what they really gave me was my life."

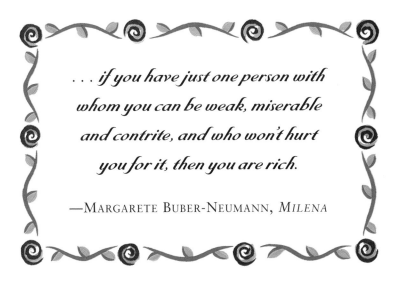

. . . if you have just one person with whom you can be weak, miserable and contrite, and who won't hurt you for it, then you are rich.

—MARGARETE BUBER-NEUMANN, *MILENA*

A Class Apart

C ynthia thought it was her very own idea.

However, in replaying her mental memory tape as she drove home, Cynthia realized that maybe it had all started with Sylvia.

Best friend Sylvia. Constant confidante Sylvia.

There was no question that at lunch today Sylvia had made some cutting remarks. It made Cynthia shiver just to think of Sylvia saying them. . . . "You've got such a great career.... I know he's smart, but where is the guy going? ... You've been married twenty-seven years; don't you think you've given James more than a chance? ... Everybody knows you—you've always been on a fast track.... He's a dead end...." And then the absolute clincher: "Is he *that* good in bed?"

Maybe it was that last question that really planted the forbidden thought in her mind. She wouldn't admit it aloud, not even to her best friend, but James was not a world-class lover. Still, that wasn't a reason either to stay in or to leave a marriage so far as she was concerned. Look, her first husband, the one from the ten-minute marriage, had been truly a great lover, and a lot of good that had done. He had walked out before their first anniversary, left her pregnant and penniless. She'd gone to work then, made a life for herself at the bank, met James, and even though his career in finance hadn't soared, he'd been steady and faithful. And she knew the value of that. Of course, when she got that third promotion at the bank, and he had received none, it grew too uncomfortable for all concerned, so he left to start his own consulting company. But the consulting company fizzled. And so had a telephone marketing service. And so had a sales job. And so had—she shook her head. She realized she couldn't remember. She had stopped keeping track somewhere in the mid-eighties.

Yet, despite the disparity in their business talents, despite his start-ups and fall-downs, despite her steady climb to the next peak, their marriage had survived.

Why is it bugging me *now?* Cynthia wondered. Is it that Sylvia is letting me know that everyone says I'm successful and he's not? And if I'm really honest with myself, if I let myself think about it, I know I'm disappointed. In him. In me. In us.

"You'd be fabulous on your own," Sylvia assured her. "Look, I'm alone, and I have a wonderful life. I see a man here and there, go to dinner with friends almost every night. A woman alone can keep her calendar as full as she wants. Plenty to do—you'll see."

Well, maybe Sylvia was right. Maybe she *should* see. By the time she arrived home, her mind was set and her anger was considerable.

"Enough," she said to James. "I can't survive with these disparate parts of my life. I'm doing fine, feeling good during the day, and I want to come home to—well, I'm not sure what I want to come home to—but I know what I don't want. I don't want to come home to this nightly depression over you and your career. So, I've been thinking about what might help. And here's my suggestion: what if I were to stay here in the city and you went to live in our house in the country?"

To her surprise, James did not protest. As she spoke, he shook his head knowingly; he seemed relieved that she had made this decision for them. The marriage was taking its toll on him, too. He was a smart man, maybe not the kind of smart that put you ahead in the business world; instead he was school smart, one of those bright guys who has a tough time once he has to earn something in life other than A's.

He actually smiled as he got into his car and drove to the country.

Cynthia, her annoyance now in check as James left, did what she soon learned many newly free, long-married women do. She enrolled in some classes she'd always wanted to take, and brought back into her life some of her old friends she'd been too married to see.

The first year was heaven. Cynthia loved every minute of her freedom. She and James spoke by phone, frequently at first and less often as time went by. Then, fourteen months after they began their separate lives, something happened. Cynthia was being considered for a senior management position, and she needed advice, the kind of advice only a family member can give. She knew her children would give advice—but they had no basis for their ideas. Only James could understand. He'd been there. He knew the cast. She told Sylvia over lunch.

"If you need him, call him," Sylvia advised, "but remember that if you do, it's an invitation to return. Do you want him back?"

"Not really," Cynthia admitted. "I'm not unhappy, but I don't know how to explain this. I just know something is missing. For the first time in twenty-seven years there's no one to share my intimate thoughts and feelings. Let's face it. Your children are your children. You love them, but who is going to tell a grown child the kind of things you tell a spouse? I miss James."

"Every time you miss him, just think of why you wanted him to leave. That will cure you," Sylvia replied curtly.

That night Cynthia stopped at a deli and bought a frozen dinner for one. She ate standing up. It didn't seem to make much sense to set the table or sit down if it meant just—just her. She picked at the food, lost in thought. I can't believe this, she told herself. I've traveled for years, stayed alone in hotels all over the world, and never once was lonely. Now, here I am at a time in life when I am more secure than ever, and I feel more insecure than ever.

She almost called to invite James home that very night.

By morning, however, her head had cleared of all such thoughts.

And so another year went by.

From time to time James phoned with news of the country house, information about things he'd read that he thought would interest Cynthia.

Then one day, with no preamble and in his usual blunt, brusque way, James suggested that they have dinner together. "Nothing too much for either of us," he explained. "You drive an hour, and I'll drive an hour. We'll meet halfway, and I will find a restaurant that I think you'll like."

Cynthia told Sylvia. "A mistake," Sylvia said. "He called you, so that means he wants to come back. You're giving him false hope. You don't want him back."

"I do, though. I do—and I don't. You're right. I'm giving him false hope. But I'm giving me false hope, too. So maybe two false make a true."

The night they were to meet, Cynthia came down with the flu. The children called and clucked sympathetically before going on to their next appointments. When James called to double-check the evening plans, Cynthia hesitated. Should she go? Should she admit that she felt rotten and wanted nothing more than to stay at home?

Well, she might not have been a good wife, but she'd always been an honest one. "I feel awful," she confessed. "I'm getting the flu or something; I don't even know what's wrong. Can we do this next week instead?"

James heard her sniffles, and from twenty-seven years of a shared life, he also heard the things she did not say. He heard "lonely," "children someplace else," "nowhere to turn."

"Stay put," he said quickly. "I'll come to you."

And so he did. He drove down from the country, and he came into her kitchen with armloads of groceries. He made soup and told stories and comforted her.

"Thank you," she said, sniffling.

"I won't bother you," he said as he kissed her goodnight on her fevered forehead. He slept in the guest room, and then, on Monday, he went back to the country.

The next weekend he came to town again. "Just to see how you're doing," he said.

James and Cynthia have had their weekend marriage for three months now. "It's not a marriage; it's not dating. What is it?" Sylvia asked one day over lunch.

"It's a relationship," Cynthia answered easily. "We go for walks and watch ball games. We don't see any old friends; we don't put any pressure on this marriage. We're too old to make a great mistake again. But I know something I've never known before. A career is not enough for me. I need intimacy. And the intimacy of women friends works best for me when I have a loving man in my life. Does that make me less of a feminist? I don't know—and guess what!—I don't care. These are my emotions we're talking about; this isn't the condiment shelf in the kitchen. I don't have to label everything.

"I have marriage. I have friendship. What else is there?"

Friendship can last between people of different sexes. . . . However, a woman always regards a man as a man, and reciprocally a man regards a woman as a woman. Such a relationship is neither passion nor pure friendship; it forms a class apart.

—JEAN DE LA BRUYÈRE, *DU COEUR, LES CARACTÈRES* . . .

Female to Female

Leslie Ann knew she had kept Sharon waiting, so she ran to the car from her house. "Sorry," she panted as she opened the car door, "but the sitter came late. I know we always try to get to Book Group on time—"

Sharon laughed. "Relax. Don't you know it's better when you never complain, never explain? Personally, I think that ought to be on every mother's refrigerator door."

Leslie Ann sighed as she sat back in her seat, buckled her belt, and settled in for the fifteen-minute drive. "I've been at home with sick children for a week, and I'm so happy to get out of the house that I babble. Sometimes I forget how grown-ups talk. Tell me what's happening in the outside world."

"Well, I had brunch yesterday with Victoria."

"Is she still in honeymoon heaven or have her feet touched ground?"

Sharon gripped the wheel. "To tell the truth, I'm worried about her. I haven't been able to stop thinking about Victoria ever since I saw her yesterday. I know you don't have a lot of time, because of the children, but try to stay in touch with Vickie. I think she's going to need her friends soon."

"Whatever are you talking about? She was so thrilled to be a married woman."

"Right. But I think she married the wrong man."

"Did she say something to you?"

"Not a word."

"Then why the worry?"

"She looks grim."

"Maybe she's tired," Sharon answered, thinking of her own weariness. "They haven't even been married a year, and she's had to get a new house ready and deal with his kids."

"No, that's a different kind of look. That's harassed. She looks grim. She married a pompous man, and she is usually so cheerful. But I think that this dreary man is getting to her."

"But she didn't say anything to you?"

"No, but she didn't have to. I can tell even by the way she walks."

"How can you be sure?"

"Because I'm her friend. Haven't you seen it, too?"

"Well, come to think of it, she's not returning calls the way she used to, and she wasn't at Book Club last month, and I asked her to go walking with me last week, and she said she was too busy. But I just figured she was putting me to one side for a while. But now that you mention it, I can see what you mean."

"Victoria is trying so hard to make things work that I don't even think she realizes what's bothering her, but she knows something is making her unhappy. When she finally puts a name to her unhappiness, believe me, she'll want us around."

A few weeks later Leslie Ann called Sharon. "I saw Victoria today."

"And?"

"And there's trouble in River City."

"Did you act surprised?"

"Of course. Don't you think I know what friends are for?"

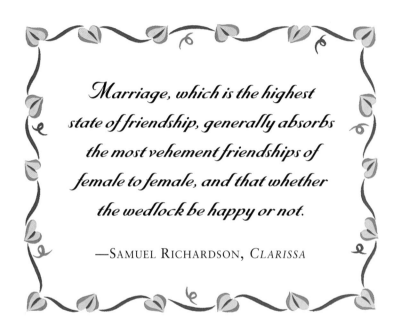

Marriage, which is the highest state of friendship, generally absorbs the most vehement friendships of female to female, and that whether the wedlock be happy or not.

—SAMUEL RICHARDSON, *CLARISSA*

Caught in the Web

Senator Floyd Haskell was determined not to let a little thing like the worst ice storm in the history of Washington keep him at home when he had a party to arrange to celebrate the fiftieth birthday of his reporter wife, Nina Totenberg.

And so the senator fearlessly opened the door that January day and stepped outside—only to hit a patch of ice and have his feet fly out from under him.

Nina Totenberg will never forget that night. She rushed to the hospital to be with her husband, who was now unconscious, and was told he needed immediate brain surgery.

Nina was scheduled to be on *ABC Nightline* that evening.

What to do?

She called Cokie Roberts, another NPR and ABC correspondent. "Fill in for me," she begged.

"I can't do the on-the-air job," Cokie told her, "because you've already filmed the interior story, and you will have to do the lead-in and lead-out. But I will fill in for you at the hospital."

And so Cokie came to the hospital while a shaken Nina went off to have a makeup person try to give her a face for the public.

When Nina returned to the hospital, Cokie was still there. So were three other friends from National Public Radio.

"It was a long night, a nightmare," Nina recalled grimly. "But they stayed; they all stayed."

The nightmare continued well beyond the next day.

Three brain operations, one bout with pneumonia, and four months later, the senator came home again.

And in between Nina and the senator learned new chapters in the book of friendship.

Never once during the entire period of the senator's hospitalization did Nina have dinner alone. From the start, her mother and sisters came to be with her. So did her husband's children and niece.

Two fellow workers fed Nina and her family three times a week.

A woman the couple knew only as party friends—the kind of acquaintances one invites to parties and is invited in return—wrote upon hearing of the accident. "I have recently retired from my job," the wife said, "and I will do anything to help—shop, chauffeur, sit."

In the end she became what Nina called her "hospital harpy," the friend who stayed at the hospital with the senator weeks after Nina went back to work, the woman who served as Nina's eyes and ears to make sure the physical therapy was progressing properly at the understaffed rehab center.

Others on the fringe of their lives came to help, too.

One arranged for a TV set to be put in Nina's bedroom, so she wouldn't be so lonesome without her husband there.

Even the First Lady's deputy chief of staff brought dinner.

Men were on call, too. A group of the senator's friends he jokingly called "the drill sergeants" came each day to lunch and exercise with him.

So what did supersavvy reporter Totenberg learn from this?

"I learned something I'd forgotten. You know, when we're in school our lives revolve around roommates, classmates, friends. But once you're out of school, it's easy to forget about the need for friends, because suddenly the world has expanded beyond the campus. There's an interesting man or an interesting job, and then, before you know it, you're swept up in a marriage or a career—or sometimes both. But maintaining friendships is not a *luxury* of life; it is a *necessity*. How could I alone have done all the things my husband needed during those months? How could I have kept his spirits up? Kept both my job and my house running if not for my friends? How could I have lived without that extra source of courage and support? It didn't matter that some of those friends who were there for us were friends we had not seen often. What mattered is that when we needed them, the tie was there. And they came to help in any way they could.

"This was a hard thing to have happen, a terrible way to learn, but because of this my friends and I are closer than ever."

*Life is a frail moth flying
Caught in the web
of the years that pass.*

SARA TEASDALE, "COME," *RIVERS TO THE SEA*

What a Pleasure

Gail was at the place she had learned to call the in-between part of life. She was young enough to hear the ticking of the biological clock and old enough to start worrying about it. Oh sure, there had been a few serious men in her life. But what had been was over. As for now, well, she certainly wasn't in love. She wasn't in like. And, as she told her friends, she wasn't even in hello.

So it was flattering when she met Larry at a dinner party one night, and he immediately complimented her and

152

engaged her in interesting, witty conversation. So she was feeling very good about herself when they sat down to dinner, Larry next to her.

"Have you met Joanne?" he asked Gail as he turned to the woman on his left. "Joanne and I live together."

Gail felt her heart go *thunk!* and she turned to talk to the man across the table.

But Larry continued to talk to Gail.

This guy is too much, Gail told herself. Coming on to me when he has already set up house with a woman. Not exactly in the best taste.

So when Larry called the next day and invited Gail to have dinner with him and Joanne, Gail said no. "I think we can be friends, all of us," he promised.

"I don't think so," Gail responded.

Despite her refusal, Larry continued to call Gail. "Just to talk," he explained.

Gail didn't really want another woman's man, but she had to admit that it was kind of flattering to get his calls. She knew, however, that she would keep him at arm's length.

A month later Larry called Gail and said, "I have some news for you. Joanne and I have split. Now will you go out with me?"

That's what Gail had been waiting to hear before giving him any encouragement. "Sure," she said.

It was no big, glamorous date, just a drink at a neighborhood pub. But Gail looked forward to talking to Larry in a new way, and she was eager to see where this might lead. But no sooner had he ordered a glass of wine than he said, "Let me tell you about Joanne and me."

Gail leaned back. Okay, she'd played the waiting game enough other times to know there was often a preamble.

But not with Larry. The preamble was the book. Larry talked and talked and talked. About Joanne.

After he took Gail home, Larry called to talk more—about Joanne.

That was when Gail picked up the phone, even though it was midnight and called her best friend. It took only five minutes for Gail to confirm what she already knew. "You're right," her friend agreed. "You are not on Larry's mind. What is on Larry's mind is his relationship with Joanne, and he isn't ready to give up talking about it."

"Well, I'm sure I've heard the last from him," Gail said to her friend.

Still, Larry called again the next night.

"Larry," Gail said as gently as she could, "I think it's too bad that you are having so many problems with Joanne, but I'm not really the one to help you. We just met. This is obviously a very difficult time for you. Don't you have any close friends with whom you can discuss this?"

"Oh yes," he said readily, "but my two best friends are really busy with their careers, and these guys just don't have time right now."

"Your two best friends aren't there for you in this crisis?" she asked, remembering her own call to her best friend the night before. "Then you ought to get yourself some new friends—and you might want to try women friends," Gail advised. "You see, when a woman is your friend, she may be too busy to listen to you that minute, but she'll call you at one A.M. or six A.M. or meet you for coffee. No woman is ever too busy to make time for a friend in trouble. You guys still don't understand how the friendship bond between women works. My friends are never too busy for me. I'm never afraid to ask them to put their careers on the back burner for an hour to hear me cry. The reason I really can't help you, Larry, is that I haven't known you long enough to know the real reason you're hurting. When you find out, call me again."

155

Six months have passed.
She still hasn't heard from Larry.

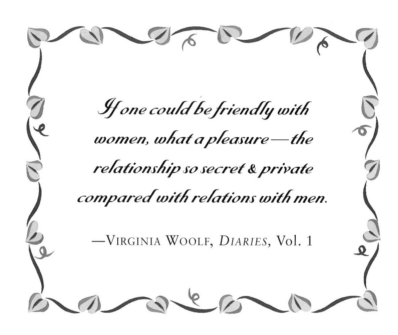

If one could be friendly with women, what a pleasure — the relationship so secret & private compared with relations with men.

—VIRGINIA WOOLF, *DIARIES*, Vol. 1

Sheer Utility

It was one of those wall-to-wall days that mothers know best. It starts behind the wheel with the car pool to school and then drives along to grocery to dry cleaner to home to video store back to school to riding lesson to library to home. It was the kind of day when Katherine referred to herself as Mom on Wheels.

On this day Katherine collected the children from school, dropped off the nonfamily riders, and was heading for home. They were a block from the house when it happened. A car sped from nowhere in a rush to make a left turn and slammed into Katherine's car just as she began to edge through the green light.

Katherine never saw the car hit. Neither did her children. But airbags opened, kids screamed, and there was blood everywhere. Both Katherine and her two children remember the sound of sirens, ambulances and a ride to the hospital.

But what Katherine remembers most is that when the accident happened, a woman appeared, as if by magic, and said, "I will go to the hospital with you. I've been through this, and you really can't be alone with the children."

And so a woman motorist who'd never met Katherine or her family went to the hospital, called Katherine's out-of-town husband and told him what had happened, stayed with the three through CAT scans and X rays, and took them home, bandaged but okay.

"How do I thank you?" Katherine mumbled shakily.

The woman shrugged. "Just be an unexpected good friend to the next person," she said.

Katherine doesn't go around looking for accidents to happen, but if one should, she'll know what to do.

If friendship is not sheer utility,

it is nonsense.

—AUSTIN O'MALLEY,
"KEYSTONES OF THOUGHT"

The Quality of Friendship

The Santa Claus on the street corner was ringing his bell, but Beth didn't have time to reach for her wallet. She was already late for work. No time for anything, she mumbled to herself as she hurried toward the office.

The Wall Street Journal was lying on her desk when she arrived, and she quickly scanned the day's big story. It was another of those Wall Street intrigues, a story of stock manipulation and the threat of the dissolution of a major financial organization. The story raised questions of responsibility and named persons under suspicion.

It was somewhere in the middle of the fourth paragraph that a name pulled out from the rest, almost as if it alone were written in capital letters.

Beth gasped.

Parker Hoyt!

Not exactly an ordinary name.

But Parker had never been an ordinary boy. She had met Parker in the second grade, and even then he had shown promise. As they went from the elementary grades to high school, each year confirmed Parker's early promise of being the boy most likely to succeed.

Then, thanks to a scholarship, he had gone on to a distinguished college career. Later, Beth followed his rise in business because his well-documented successes and promotions were recorded regularly in the financial press. Parker had certainly become the most famous member of their class.

But according to this story, his spiraling career path had led to the sinking of a megabillion-dollar company.

Beth shook her head in disbelief.

How could this have happened to Parker?

This was an old pal, a good friend. Throughout their school days Parker, Beth, and Beth's best friend, Leah, had always had a lock on top academic honors. The three had all been on the fast track, not only in class, but outside class.

And somehow their competitiveness, instead of making them enemies, had cemented their friendship.

Beth picked up the phone and called her husband, Jack. Yes, he had seen the story. Yes, he shared her shock and surprise.

All day, in and out of meetings, Beth thought of Parker.

That night at dinner with Jack, Beth fiddled with her food. "Can you believe this about Parker—Parker, of all people?" she asked.

"Other guys—maybe. Parker, no," her husband answered grimly. Jack had been two years ahead of Beth at school, had played football with Parker, and knew him well.

"His family—what can this be doing to them?" Beth asked sadly. "What kind of Christmas will it be for them?"

The next day in a financial meeting, Beth listened as a corporate officer glibly explained a balance-sheet loss by shifting the responsibility for errors to a younger person in the department.

Beth felt her back stiffen.

How many times had she sat through meetings where executives absolved themselves of any guilt in a plan gone wrong by fingerpointing a lower-echelon employee?

Could this have happened to Parker?

Why had she been so quick to assume Parker really was guilty? Wasn't this the season of goodwill? Why had she thought ill instead of good? What if . . .

Beth knew what she had to do. After the meeting she picked up the telephone and called Parker. "Need a friend?" she asked.

"Yes," he answered simply.

"Let's meet for lunch tomorrow."

Across the luncheon table Parker said, "I suppose you want to know what happened."

"No, I don't," she answered truthfully.

"Thank you." There was an audible sigh of relief. "The attorneys have told me not to discuss anything with anyone."

"But let's talk about you and how you're feeling," Beth said. "Has anyone called you?"

"Just you and Leah."

"Leah?" Beth gasped. "Where is she? I haven't heard from her in ten years. We both got so busy, and—"

"We all did," Parker added solemnly. "But here's her phone number. She lives outside San Francisco."

Beth called Leah that night, and for three hours they talked. They expressed their surprise at Parker's dilemma and each pledged to lend her support.

"In the spirit of Christmas," Beth said.

"And in the spirit of friendship," Leah added.

Leah told Beth that she was now married, the mother of two children, and worked for a bank.

As they spoke, Beth felt the years slide away. They were teenagers again with stories of their lives. "Oh, I've missed you so," she said to Leah. And Leah confessed that she thought of Beth often, but never knew just how to reach her.

By the time they finished talking, they had each promised never again to let this distance and time separate them.

When Beth finally crawled into bed that night, she told Jack all the details of her long talk.

Then, as they were ready for sleep, she reached for her husband and held him close. "Christmas always makes me feel kind of sad and happy when I think of what life really is and how hard it is for so many people. I guess it will really be tough for Parker, but I wonder if I'd have called him if I hadn't sort of felt a Christmas spirit and my own need to help someone in need. And now, because I did, I have darling Leah back in my life. It's like an incredible present."

"We don't always buy the things that matter most," Jack said softly. "I'm glad you called Parker. I will, too."

"I thought you probably would. But, Jack dear, don't you think that of all the people who knew Parker it's kind of surprising that only Leah and I called—"

"Not surprising at all," Jack whispered as he held his wife close. "I've got my arms around my best friend, so I learned years ago that women make the best friends."

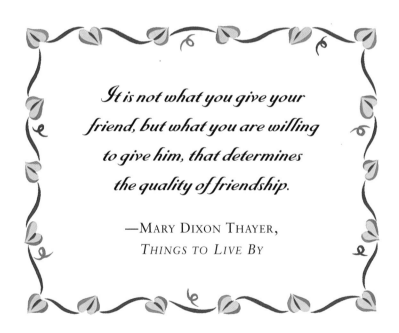

It is not what you give your friend, but what you are willing to give him, that determines the quality of friendship.

—MARY DIXON THAYER, *THINGS TO LIVE BY*

The Poetry of Life

She was my oldest and dearest friend.

"We went to school together, and we had daughters around the same ages. When either of us had a problem with our girls, we'd call the other for advice.

"I guess some women do their best confessing over a martini or a back fence. For us it was always a meeting at the soda shop where we'd share our secrets over a Reese's Pieces sundae.

"When Ellie became ill, really ill, she told me over a Reese's Pieces sundae. And when the cancer came back a few years later, and she was in the hospital, her daughter and I went to see her. 'What I really want more than anything,' Ellie said, 'is a Reese's Pieces sundae.'

"Her daughter went out and got us two, and we laughed together over our sundaes.

"It was the last time.

"She died the next afternoon."

—A NEW YORK HOUSEWIFE

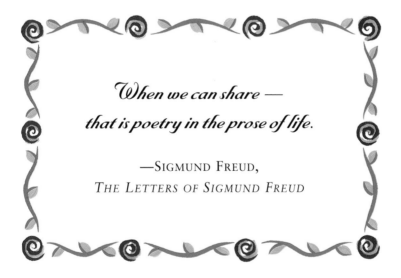

When we can share —

that is poetry in the prose of life.

—SIGMUND FREUD,
THE LETTERS OF SIGMUND FREUD

Elemental Forces

When Sandra heard the news, she couldn't believe it.

She immediately called Sara.

"Incredible," Sara said, and called Laura.

And then Laura called Roseanne. "We want to take you to lunch," she said softly. "We feel terrible."

Of course Laura hadn't yet discussed lunch with the other girls, but—well, how could they say no?

"The bastard," Sandra said.

"A son of a bitch," Sara added.

"I could believe it of him. But her? Her?" Now it was Laura's turn.

Roseanne sighed. "It's the oldest story in the world, only I never thought it would happen to me."

"You were so good to him," Sandra said.

"The best," Sara echoed.

"Why? Why?" Laura asked.

"I knew about the girl at the office," Roseanne said grimly. "I think the whole town knew, and I needed to talk to someone. I just had to vent, to get rid of my anger and think it through. I knew I didn't want to throw my marriage away, and besides, I was sure he'd never marry a girl from the office. It would be so—so out of character for him, if you know what I mean. At lunch one day with Barbara, I just broke down and confided my fears to her. I told her the whole story, and Barbara was absolutely darling to me. She even offered to go to Lawrence and talk to him."

"Why didn't *you* confront him?" Laura asked.

"Because if I accused him, and he wasn't guilty, I'd have put a terrible thing between us. And who wants to look like a wife who doesn't trust her husband? There'd be no place for our marriage to go. Well, Barbara certainly agreed with me."

"I'll bet she did," Sandra said sarcastically.

"So that's how Barbara got to him," Sara said slowly.

Roseanne nodded. "She was really trying to do a good thing. She went to Lawrence, and she explained that she loved me very much, and she noticed that I was looking drawn and sad and had asked me what the problem was. And when I said I was worried about him and his feelings, he told her that it was true; he was feeling very sad about our life. So then Barbara came back to me and suggested I take some courses and get my hair colored and change my makeup. But I told her, this is the way I am, and this is what he bought—so he'd better settle down. Then, just to show me that I could make changes, she did. She enrolled in a computer course—you know, Lawrence is into computers—and she had her hair colored, and she even had her colors done. You know, that silly business where some expert tells you whether you're a spring or winter or fall personality and what colors you should wear. Well, she did it all just to show me how easy it was. She did it all trying to save me."

"And that's when Lawrence noticed her," Laura added.

"But she did it out of friendship," Roseanne protested.

"I still can't believe Lawrence left you for Barbara," Sara said. "It's just too much, and we want you to know that we all feel awful, just awful about this. We'll do anything you want. We'll never speak to him again—or we will, just depending on whatever you want. This is all so horrible."

"I thought it was a good marriage. Twelve years. Twelve years," Roseanne repeated. "And now I'm alone."

"It's so awful," Laura said. "I know you must feel lonely."

Roseanne looked at her friends. "Yes, I do," she admitted. "I feel very lonely."

"It's hard for women like us without a man," Sara said. "Lawrence was such a presence in your life."

"Oh, it isn't Lawrence I was thinking of," Roseanne told her friends. "It's Barbara I miss. She's the one who was always there to talk with me."

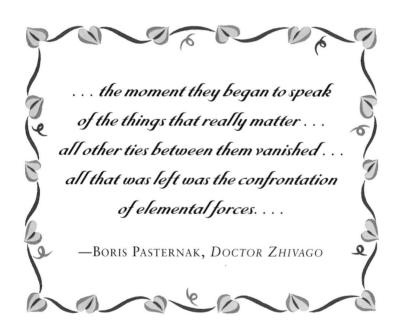

> . . . the moment they began to speak
> of the things that really matter . . .
> all other ties between them vanished . . .
> all that was left was the confrontation
> of elemental forces. . . .
>
> —BORIS PASTERNAK, *DOCTOR ZHIVAGO*

Immortality

Ihave an old-fashioned hobby in a souped-up world.

I collect letters.

You remember letters? They are what we once sent, not to pay bills and complain of service, but to make appointments and arrangements for life.

The letters I collect are those of twentieth-century writers, and when the world is too much with me, I go to the wall of my library and look at Edith Wharton's letter to a friend promising to send her carriage for their visit the next day. Or I read Edna St. Vincent Millay's handwritten note appended to the Christmas card she sent to Mrs. Robinson Jeffers. And what is the significance of those long-ago letters to my life today? Well, for one thing they cause me to pause before I reach for the phone. And sometimes I even reach for a pen instead.

The difference between a call and a letter is the difference between the life worth saving and the disposable life. Besides, a letter is the ultimate old-fashioned courtesy between friends, since, unlike the telephone, it never rings and rings, interrupting the flow of life and demanding immediate attention. A letter offers the recipient the luxury of choosing the time and space to add it to her life.

And a letter, unlike a phone call, can be read and reread. It calms and soothes the sometimes turbulent waters of friendship. A letter, once a part of the writer, now becomes a part of the recipient. Outside of our actual presence, it is the best physical proof we can offer of our friendship, our care and concern for another.

Write a letter, and you secure your place in the quilting bee. You are a spinner of stories once again, a recaller of memories, a maker of dreams.

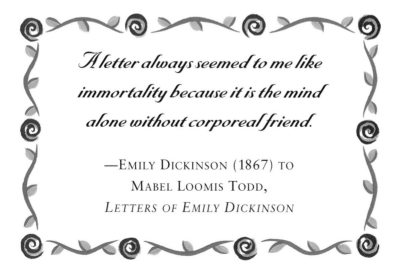

A letter always seemed to me like immortality because it is the mind alone without corporeal friend.

—EMILY DICKINSON (1867) TO
MABEL LOOMIS TODD,
LETTERS OF EMILY DICKINSON

Small Talk

I really appreciate your having the Brysons come over to watch the game tonight," Eddie said to Rita on Sunday afternoon as they worked side by side in the kitchen making a pot of coffee and assembling a tray of cold cuts.

"It's okay with me," Rita said, nibbling a slice of turkey, "but I feel a little funny. I mean, I never even met her, and now I have to spend a whole afternoon with her."

"Well, he said his wife hates football, and I said you did, too, and maybe you girls could go to a movie, and we'd watch the game together, and you know—"

"—I know he's new at the office, and you want a chance to get to know him."

"You got the picture, and I appreciate it."

"Okay. Okay. Just remember—you owe me one."

He kissed her. "First payment on the debt."

She laughed. "It's not what I had in mind, but I'll take it."

Seven hours later, Eddie and Rita were in the kitchen once again, this time wrapping leftovers and loading the dishwasher.

"He's a good guy."

"Oh? How do you know?" Rita asked.

"Well, he's just a regular guy. He likes football, and we talked about the teams. He played in college. He's just easy. What did you think of her?"

"I like her. We talked a lot."

"Well, what can I expect when two women get together? Okay, what did you learn?"

"For starters, do you know that she's a cousin of the chairman?"

"Oh my God. No."

"Do you know that he was in Vietnam and was wounded

and had a rough time getting his life together, and this is his second marriage?"

"Really?"

"He has two kids from the first marriage. It's her second also."

"And all I found out was that he played football in college. All right. What else did you find out?"

"That's about it. Except her cousin the chairman is more like a brother to her, and they talk all the time, and she was really curious to meet you."

"How do women learn so much so fast?"

"Well, darling, we drove to the movies, so we had twenty minutes all to ourselves. And the thing about women is that we don't ask those usual where-were-you-born questions. Women talk about feelings. And all I asked was, 'So how do you feel about leaving your home and moving? Isn't that hard on the family?' And then—well, to tell you the truth, she started to talk. So I parked at the movie theater, and pretty soon we realized we'd missed the start of the picture, so we decided that we'd rather talk than see a movie, so we went into the coffee shop in town, and that's where we were until it was time to come back here."

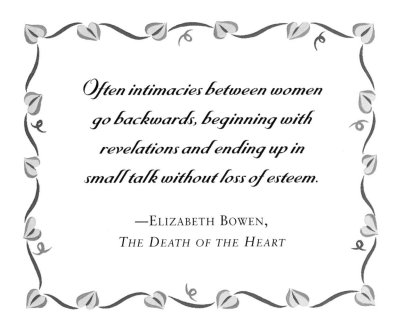

Often intimacies between women go backwards, beginning with revelations and ending up in small talk without loss of esteem.

—Elizabeth Bowen,
The Death of the Heart

Very Rare and Very Precious

M y mother was born in New York City, and her family moved to Cleveland when she was a baby.

Not long after that she made her first friend, Bena.

My grandparents' house became Bena's second home as the two young girls grew up together. When in the elementary grades, they delivered meat to the customers of my grandfather's butcher shop during lunchtime and after school. When they were little, they teased their older sisters. Later they went to Central High together, where they quickly learned that the way to leave the building was through the door where the boys were. After graduation they both went to work (Mother was a secretary at the Board of Education), and their weekend treat was to meet at Hoffman's at East 105th and Euclid where they gossiped over hot fudge sundaes. When they were nineteen, the two girls went to a Halloween party where they met the two boys who would become their husbands.

As young wives they saw less of each other, but there was always a bond between them. It was not until both were widowed and living alone that their friendship began to flower once again.

They met for lunch, for cards, and exchanged vital statistics about children, grandchildren, and then great-grandchildren.

A couple of years ago, at the insistence of her children, Bena moved to an apartment complex designed for people over sixty.

"Do you want to go?" we asked my mother.

"Definitely not," she said. "I want my independence."

So we said no more. At ninety, my mother was still well-read, chic, and able to parallel-park at the mall.

But after a tough midwestern winter marked by a series of blizzards and an electrical outage at her apartment house that left her isolated on the fifth floor without elevator service, wiser heads prevailed.

Mother moved.

Yes, she went to the same apartment complex as Bena.

The first time I visited Mother, she said Bena was coming to see me, too. Why not? She'd been coming to see me since the day I was born.

"We giggle a lot together," my mother told me after Bena arrived.

"We remember a lot of things nobody knows," Bena reported.

"Once, when we were little, I took Bena's sister's hat, and she took my sister's hat. We can't remember why, but we still laugh about it." Mother was still laughing as she retold the story.

And as I looked at my mother, secure, snug and still smiling with her old friend in her new apartment, I realized how much of my life Mother has shaped.

It was my mother who led me to my first friend, and now my mother has lived to show me the ultimate truth—that all friends are not for life, but if you have a true friend, you have a life.

Friendship is very rare, my dear, & very precious, & grows rarer & more precious. . . .

—JOHN MASEFIELD, *LETTERS TO REYNA*

Acknowledgments

I never thought it would happen, but I married my best friend.

Lee became my best friend not long after my first marriage ended, and I ran into him—literally—on the street. We'd known each other for years but hadn't seen each other for a while. He asked all the usual what's-new stuff, and when I told him the news of me, he was disbelieving, but after I explained that yes, it was all true and I was free, he said that he'd been through this. He put his hand on my arm, a comforting gesture that I was to learn later was as natural to him as nodding yes or no. It was his way of saying, I understand. He acknowledged that this must be a tough time for me; he remembered his own pain in similar circumstances. Then he invited me to a dinner party he was giving and, almost as an afterthought, added that maybe I'd like to go to his house the day before the party and cook with him.

I was aware that Lee was as well known for his cooking as his life in the theater, so I quickly said yes.

From then on I became the sous-chef in his life. It was a lot of cutting and paring and scraping. I learned how to fillet fish and handle phyllo, and I must have pounded a few carloads of chicken breasts during the two years of our seeing each other.

By the time we married, we knew each other well. We could talk together or read alone. We could stay in or go out. All that mattered was that we did whatever we did together. He told one of his best friends, a woman, that the reason he planned to marry me was that he wanted us to go on just as we were, and he felt that if we didn't marry and give our friendship a place to grow, we would lose it.

And so we both gained the best times, the best love of our lives. Lee was always willing to admit that, just as I was willing to tell him.

We both knew, although I don't think we ever said it to each other, that good love begins with friendship. But this we did say—that in order for our love to grow, we would always give each other freedom, time, and emotional support.

We kept that pledge every day of our life together.

Only a few years into our marriage we learned that Lee had brain cancer. I didn't want to believe what was happening. He was more accepting than I, but he wanted so much to live. In a letter to a friend after his first surgery, he wrote, "The doctors have done their work, and now it looks as if I'll either live forever or die soon. Frankly I prefer the former."

He fought hard to make that happen, but there are some battles nobody wins. This was one of those no-win fights. But, oh, Lee was a beautiful fighter.

My husband died Sunday, March 27, 1988, at 9:08 A.M., and I remember the minute because at that moment I thought that my life had ended, too.

I had lost not only my husband but my best friend. I always knew his true worth.

In short order, however, I learned the true worth of all my best friends when I turned to them. Or, to be totally accurate, my best friends turned to me. They turned and offered sheltering arms, companionship, sympathetic ears, and a love that made no demands.

They were there in 1988.

They were there before 1988.

They were there before I even knew Lee.

They are still there.

And there are new friends, too, friends who never even met Lee.

Any life worth living has this layering of friends, this support system of loving friends.

We need our friends both for everyday living and the accidents of life: illness, broken bones, broken homes, lost loves. Widowhood is another in the list of accidents. None of us plans to become a widow. It's one of those things—like finding your first gray hair or seeing a wrinkle—one of those life events you assume will happen to somebody else but not you.

And certainly not to me and our perfect marriage.

How could I have survived that terrible time and rebuilt my life without my loving friends?

My loving friends. These words are like a mantra for me.

And not just me. For all of us, whether we walk old paths or blaze new trails, friends remain important.

Even when we do not live in expectation of marriage, we cannot get by without friendship.

Friendship is a marriage of sorts anyway. It's a choice, a commitment, a promise to fulfill.

And so this book is written to celebrate that spirit of friendship that thrives in sunlight and can be seen in darkness. It is for the women who are always there, the men who are often there. But mostly it is because friendship has long been the secret of women; men are just beginning to understand how we do it.

This book is written for anyone who ever said "I couldn't have made it without my friends," and it is dedicated to the friends whose continuing love has sustained me. There are the friends of my childhood and early years in Cleveland, friends of my New York years, friends I have met all over the world, and the friends who shared the stories in this book.

I am grateful to Phyllis Cerf Wagner, whose thoughtful advice and devoted friendship helped me get this book on track and who gave me the confidence to say what my heart whispered. I also thank Carolyn Reidy, who believed it was time to talk about friendship and who was there to guide and inspire from idea to finished book; Laurie Bernstein, whose commitment and editorial input were invaluable; my partners and loving friends, Helene Silver and Patricia Rosenwald; Annelle Warwick Savitt and Phyllis Levy, for sharing their ideas and just being there; and Owen Laster for his guidance and interest. Thanks are also due to others of my close friends: Marianne Gogolick and Eva Pusta, longtime confidantes; Sheilah Rae, my theater partner; Corky Ribakoff and Hope Gropper, whose roots intertwine with mine. And a special word of appreciation to John Mack Carter, whose humor, wisdom, and professional and personal kindnesses give friendship its true meaning.

I am thankful each day that my life is blessed by the sweet love and friendship of Lee's children and mine and of my special nephew, as well.

Each of these people, plus a cast that would make Lee proud, has made it possible for my life to go on and for me to continue the habit of loving.

. . . because a good marriage is based on the talent for friendship.

—Nietzsche, *Human, All-Too-Human*